THE ARAB REDISCOVERY OF EUROPE

IBRAHIM ABU-LUGHOD

THE ARAB REDISCOVERY OF EUROPE

A Study in Cultural Encounters

SAQI

ISBN 978-0-86356-403-1

First published by Princeton University Press in 1963
This new edition published by Saqi Books in 2011

A full cip record for this book is available from the British Library.
A full cip record for this book is available from the Library of Congress.

Printed and bound by CPI Mackays, Chatham, ME5 8TD

SAQI
26 Westbourne Grove, London W2 5RH
www.saqibooks.com

Contents

Introduction to this New Edition by Rashid Khalidi 7

Preface 15

Introduction: The Setting of Westernization 18

1. Arab Awareness of the West: Modern Beginnings 27
   - The Napoleonic Proclamations 28
   - The Arab Chroniclers of the French Expedition 35

2. The Development of the Translation Movement 43
   - The Period of Unorganized Official Interpreting 45
   - The Period of Random Translation, 1826–1835 46
   - Organized Period of Official Translation, 1835–1848 54
   - The Decline of Official Translation, 1849–1863 56
   - Revival of the Translation Movement and its Shift in Focus 57

3. The Nature of the Translated Material 60
   - Translations Undertaken 61
   - List of Translations 63
   - The Content of the Translations 67
   - Other Translators of the Nineteenth Century 70
   - A Digression on the Ninth- and Nineteenth-Century Translation 71
   - Justifications for the Translations 72
   - The Impact of the Translations on Arab Intellectual Development 75

4. Arab Travellers to Europe 78
Pre-Nineteenth-Century Travellers 79
Nineteenth-Century Travellers 81
Nineteenth-Century Travel Accounts 83
The Subject Matter of the Travel Books 88
Impact of the Travels 91

5. Travellers' Views of Europe: Political and Social Organization 97
The Political Organization of the State 98
Private Organizations 116

6. Travellers' Views of Europe: The Educational System and the Social Order 123
Education and Learning 123
Miscellaneous Sociological Observations 132

7. Arab Attitudes and Reactions to Western Achievements 141
Statements of Individual Writers 143
Reactions to the Invidious Comparisons 150

8. Conclusions and Subsequent Developments 160

Bibliography 173

Index 183

Introduction to this New Edition

Rashid Khalidi

Originally written over sixty years ago, and first published a few years later, in 1963, *The Arab Rediscovery of Europe* is both a brilliant artifact of its era, and a work well ahead of its time. For both reasons, it repays a careful reading, and its reappearance in print is long overdue and very welcome.

Produced as a doctoral dissertation in what was then the Department of Oriental Studies at Princeton University in 1957, this book is a good reflection of the state of the discipline at that time. One of the first important works of what today would be considered modern Middle Eastern intellectual history, it came out of a department that, like a few others in American and European universities, covered topics spanning the entire history and civilization of the Near East, including the nearly six millennia from the dawn of written history until the modern era. *The Arab Rediscovery of Europe* shows the text-based emphasis and the concern for language and philology characteristic of such departments, of which Princeton's at the time was one of the most distinguished.

This book is thus an example of the best and most rigorous type of Oriental studies. This field was the subject of the famous work *Orientalism* by Ibrahim Abu-Lughod's close friend, Edward Said, which was published fifteen years later.[1] The two men first met at Princeton while Said was a young undergraduate with little interest in or knowledge of scholarship on the Middle East, and Abu-Lughod was an advanced graduate student, working on the dissertation that formed the core of this book. Their friendship and intellectual

1. New York: Random House, 1978.

interaction were central in the lives of both men, and with this book one can discern the beginning of their mutual influence on one another. It is clear from published interviews with both that Said's treatment of many of the problems he dealt with so masterfully in *Orientalism* grew in large measure out of what he learned from Ibrahim Abu-Lughod over a number of years regarding a field about which he initially knew little.

While Ibrahim Abu-Lughod benefited from this rigorous training in languages and in the reading and analysis of texts, he was far from being a traditional Orientalist. Indeed, his book embodied several important and entirely new emphases. One was its exclusive focus on the Arab world, rather than on Islam or the larger Ottoman Near East: thus it lays stress on developments among thinkers and writers in the Arab countries in particular. Another is its focus on Arab authors and political figures who were progressives, constitutionalists and democrats. Against a background of scholarly work which until that time portrayed the intellectual milieu in the region as characterized by stagnation and decline, and which saw the sources of change in this dismal picture as coming almost entirely from the direct inspiration of reforming Western diplomats, missionaries and educators,[1] Abu-Lughod's book constitutes a nuanced and forceful corrective which has been fully upheld by subsequent research.

The Arab Rediscovery of Europe also marks the beginning of an emphasis on the modern Middle East as a field of study, and a focus on intellectual history and the history of ideas in the Middle East. In this it can be paired with Albert Hourani's *Arabic Thought in the Liberal Age*, which was written later than Abu-Lughod's dissertation, but was published one year earlier.[2] Ironically, neither author was aware of the work of the other when they wrote.[3] The stress of both books on intellectual history and their definition of a new field

1. A typical example was Sir Harold Temperley's *England and the Near East: The Crimea*, London, 1936, which misleadingly gave most of the credit for Ottoman reform efforts of the mid-nineteenth century to the British Ambassador in Istanbul, Sir Stratford Canning.

2. Cambridge: Cambridge University Press, 1962.

3. Personal information of the author from Ibrahim Abu-Lughod and Albert Hourani.

were the hallmarks of much scholarship in subsequent years. They were highly influential in laying out lines of further inquiry, and in establishing benchmarks for later research. In a sense, with these interventions Abu-Lughod and Hourani helped to establish the parameters within which the study of the history of the modern Arab world was to develop subsequently. They thus played a crucial role in the institutionalization of the study of the modern Middle East, which has thrived over the intervening decades.

Like most other works of this period, Abu-Lughod's *The Arab Rediscovery of Europe* is deeply marked by the impact of modernization theory, which was highly influential in the social sciences in the 1950s and 1960s, and also by a set of related assumptions about progress and Westernization. In line with these assumptions, Abu-Lughod attempts to examine, in different ways, how Arab thinkers in the nineteenth century and afterwards reacted to and interacted with Western ideas, and how they responded to the growing power of European states in the Arab world. In this respect, he also blazed a trail for many subsequent studies. To a far greater degree than earlier scholars, Abu-Lughod, like Albert Hourani, showed a marked sensitivity to the impact of the writers and ideas discussed on the more recent history and politics of the Arab world.

This sensitivity was the result of a number of factors. One was the fact that both scholars had active lives outside the academy, and had traveled and lived extensively in the Middle East. Thus Ibrahim Abu-Lughod had grown up in Palestine, lived in Egypt and elsewhere in the Arab world, and was a prominent figure in Palestinian and Arab political and cultural arenas for much of his life; while Hourani had taught in Beirut in the late 1930s, served in the British Foreign Service in Cairo during World War II, and thereafter worked for the Arab Office in Jerusalem. It may also derive from the fact that Abu-Lughod and Hourani were among the first generation of scholars of Middle Eastern origin to teach about the Middle East in leading North American and European universities. In this regard, they followed in the footsteps of pioneers like Philip Hitti, who taught at Princeton from 1926 to 1954. This towering figure in the field clearly influenced Abu-Lughod, who, while at Princeton, took Hitti's seminar, which closely analyzed seminal Arabic historical texts.[1] However, in his writings Ibrahim Abu-Lughod dealt much more directly with modern and contemporary aspects of developments in the Middle East than did Hitti, a prolific scholar whose published work ranged from ancient Near Eastern history to medieval Islamic and Arab history.

In *The Arab Rediscovery of Europe*, Abu-Lughod begins from the assumption – which was prevalent in contemporary and much subsequent scholarship – that the Middle East had been in "decline" for many centuries leading up to the nineteenth century. This was understood not only as a diminution in the capabilities of Middle Eastern states – which in fact was definitely the case by comparison with the sixteenth or seventeenth centuries – but rather as an uninterrupted, across the board process of deterioration in their societies and economies, and in intellectual life. Clearly, in none of these spheres could the Middle East (or most other parts of the world) compare with the rapid advances in the expanding, industrializing and modernizing societies and states of Western Europe. However, many authors were misled by a combination of what appeared to be the unquestionable relative decline of the Ottoman Empire *vis-à-vis* the West, a focus on what was happening at the level of the central government and the machinery of state to the detriment of study of the provincial peripheries and the rest of society, and an over-reliance on the observations of not always reliable contemporary Western visitors to the Middle East. This led them to go beyond this to describe a bleak picture of social, economic, intellectual, and political stagnation, backwardness and decline. Among the most influential of these scholars were H. A. R. Gibb and Harold Bowen, who laid out the most complete version of this analysis in their classic work *Islamic Society and the West*, which Abu-Lughod cites.[2] Gibb was the acknowledged doyen of Islamic studies at Oxford until 1955, when he

1. Personal information from the Abu-Lughod family.
2. *Islamic Society and the West: A Study of the Impact of Western Civilization on Moslem Culture in the Near East*, Oxford: Oxford University Press, Vol. I, parts 1 and 2, 1950 and 1957.

moved to Harvard. There he continued to train students who have had a considerable influence on the field down to the present day.

Scholarship published in recent decades, based largely on research from the Ottoman archives (which were not yet catalogued or fully available at the time when Gibb and Bowen or Abu-Lughod were writing) and on other rich sources like the archives of the Shari'a courts, has enabled historians to draw a much fuller and more nuanced picture of developments in Middle Eastern society and intellectual life. An example of this is Roger Owen's seminal article, published a decade after *The Arab Rediscovery of Europe*, which critiqued the received version of the status of this society.[1] Later work, notably by the great historian of the Arab city, André Raymond, has given considerable substance to Owen's more complex analysis,[2] in contradistinction to the traditional view put forward by Gibb and Bowen. However, all of this was well into the future when Ibrahim Abu-Lughod wrote *The Arab Rediscovery of Europe*. In his book, Abu-Lughod was understandably respectful of the great scholarship and erudition of Gibb and the earlier generation of scholars of Oriental Studies, even if his work went well beyond theirs in several important ways.

In another important respect, moreover, Abu-Lughod was well ahead of his time. *The Arab Rediscovery of Europe* shows that, much earlier than most others, he had detected the biases in and the faulty basis of the views on the modern Middle East held by Bernard Lewis, who has been described by one of his students as "the most influential postwar historian of Islam and the Middle East".[3] More than a decade after Ibrahim Abu-Lughod left the Department of

1. The article was entitled "The Middle East in the Eighteenth Century: An 'Islamic' Society in Decline? A Critique of Gibb and Bowen's *Islamic Society and the West*," *Review of Middle Eastern Studies*, 1 (1976) also published in the *Bulletin* of the British Society for Middle East Studies, vol. 3, no. 2, (1976), 110–117.

2. Notably in *The Great Arab Cities in the Sixteenth to Eighteenth Centuries: An Introduction*, New York: New York University Press, 1984; *Grandes villes arabes à l'époque ottomane*, Paris: Sindbad, 1985; and in detail in the articles collected in *Arab Cities in the Ottoman Period*, Aldershot: Ashgate, 2002. Owen was a student of Albert Hourani, who himself had been a student of Gibb's.

3. Martin Kramer, "Bernard Lewis," *Encyclopedia of Historians and Historical Writing*, London: Fitzroy Dearborn, 1999, p. 719.

Oriental Studies at Princeton, Lewis would arrive there to take up a chair in what had by then become the Department of Near East Studies. Lewis came to dominate Middle East studies at Princeton, where he eventually effaced almost entirely the influence of Philip Hitti and his colleagues and students. Lewis' shadow still looms there today, long after his retirement in 1986, but his considerable impact on attitudes towards the Middle East goes far beyond the precincts of Princeton University. Even more significantly, Lewis has profoundly influenced American policy and public discourse on the Middle East, lending his considerable authority to public views that are insidiously inimical to Islam and the Arabs, with works like *What Went Wrong: the Clash between Islam and Modernity*,[1] essays like "The Roots of Muslim Rage,"[2] and speeches at right-wing venues in the United States and Israel.

Ibrahim Abu-Lughod was already aware of these biases when he worked on his dissertation at Princeton. His careful reading of a range of works by Lewis that bore directly on the topics covered by *The Arab Rediscovery of Europe* revealed a striking inattention on Lewis' part to the nuances of the texts he referred to, and a troubling tendency to oversimplify and generalize.

Abu-Lughod takes issue with Lewis' interpretations in particular in the two longest footnotes in the book. Thus in an extremely cogent response to the sweeping statement by Lewis that the Arabic word *jumhuriyya* "is an innovation of the late nineteenth century", and was not used to denote a "republic" until then, Abu-Lughod shows convincingly, with extensive reference to a number of key texts, that in fact the Arabic term was in wide use by a number of the most important authors in the Arabic language several decades before that.[3] This raises the question of whether Lewis had a mastery of (or had even read) some of the seminal works by figures as crucial for the development of Arab and Muslim views of Europe and the West as Rifa'a Rafi' al-Tahtawi and Khayr al-Din al-Tunisi, or was simply relying on his broad knowledge of late Ottoman sources.

1. Oxford: Oxford University Press, 2001.
2. *The Atlantic*, September, 1990.
3. *The Arab Rediscovery of Europe*, n. 2, pp. 32–33.

Abu-Lughod's tone towards "Professor Lewis" is naturally respectful, but this lengthy digression makes it clear that it is worrisome to him, and is meant to worry the reader, that an authority like Lewis could have been so mistaken regarding a political term of such importance and used by such significant authors.

The second instance where Abu-Lughod takes issue with Lewis for making broad and unsubstantiated assertions comes with regard to a topic perhaps more troubling than that of the first use of the Arabic term for "republic" in the Arabic sources, important though that was. This relates to Lewis' assertion in more than one context that the French Revolution was attractive to Muslims because it was secular. The implication is that because the revolution "freed France and her achievements from an association with Christianity," it was possible for Muslims to view the West positively for the first time. Abu-Lughod states in another lengthy footnote that his investigation of the "chief sources" of the Arab and Muslim reaction to France after the revolution – one of the main topics treated in *The Arab Rediscovery of Europe* – does not in any way substantiate Lewis' view. He proceeds to show that the contrary was the case: if anything, these writers were disturbed by the lack of French "religious ardor." Abu-Lughod suggests that this serious error could have been a result of Lewis' reliance on a few Ottoman sources, although he notes that even for the Ottoman context this claim has been questioned by the preeminent authority on the subject, Şerif Mardin.[1]

These apparently minor matters take on importance in view of the ponderous and repeated pronouncements that Lewis, originally known as a medievalist and an Ottomanist, made during the latter part of his lengthy career about the modern Arab and Muslim worlds. If in fact his evidence was flawed on basic matters such as these relating to the nineteenth century, if he engaged in a careless reading of the sources, and if the foundations of his judgments were consequently unsound, that is all the more reason to doubt his sweeping conclusions about why the Arabs do or say this or that in the modern world. In other words, long before Edward Said's critique

1. Ibid., n. 2, p. 141.

of Lewis in *Orientalism*, his close friend and mentor Ibrahim Abu-Lughod had turned up detailed evidence of troubling, fundamental errors in the work of this renowned savant.

There are many reasons for turning again to *The Arab Rediscovery of Europe* so long after its original publication. It is characterized by fine-grained scholarship, an attentive and close reading of seminal texts, and by respect for and careful explication of the context of these writings by the first and most eminent authors in the modern era to attempt to understand Europe from the vantage point of the Arab world, and to try to chart out a new course for their region. All these features make it an essential work for understanding the changes that have been underway in the Middle East since the late eighteenth century. Beyond that, it has attained the status of a modern classic, and represents a milestone in the growth of the thriving field of modern Middle Eastern history. We are fortunate that with this new edition it can be easily accessible to scholars and students alike.

October 2010
Columbia University

Preface

The theme of this book is modern Arab awareness of the West, which began in embryonic form when the French forces under Napoleon occupied Egypt in 1798. The study traces the growth of that awareness and examines the works of Arab writers who helped to formulate a new image of the West and to shape Arab response to the challenge raised by cultural contact between disparate worlds. This volume treats developments up to 1870, which marked the opening of the second phase of literary revival. Subsequent developments have been reserved for a separate work.

To describe Arab awareness of the West and to explore the major channels through which western ideas were transmitted to the Arab world, three main literary sources were utilized, each of which is dealt with in a separate section of this book. The first part is devoted to an analysis of sources dealing with the Napoleonic expedition itself, primarily the explanations and interpretations of Arab chroniclers. From their writings it is clear that western facts and concepts – inaccurately learned and ill-understood by the writers themselves – were being inscribed on a virtual *tabula rasa*.

This faltering beginning, however, gathered greater facility and sophistication during the ensuing decades. Muhammad 'Ali's assumption of power in Egypt signified a tremendous growth in Arab awareness of and appreciation for the West. Among the numerous methods he used to create a strong state modelled on western lines was the translation of western, mainly French, books into the Arabic language. Chapters II and III discuss the genesis and growth of the translation movement and analyze the nature of the material translated to show how this movement contributed to the growing Arab awareness of the West.

Muhammad ʿAli, however, was not alone in his endeavors. Many individual Arabs were gradually developing an interest in Europe which led to travel abroad. A number of them wrote accounts of their journeys, incorporating not only descriptive information but also comments on the social, educational, and political institutions of Europe. These accounts constitute a significant method by which western ideology was transmitted to an increasingly receptive Arab audience. Chapters IV, V, and VI identify these travellers, describe their works, and indicate the impressions Europe made on them.

In Chapter VII the reactions of translators and travellers to western phenomena and ideas are analyzed. While their reactions, in general, were quite favorable, one sees foreshadowed the basic lines of later polemics. The final chapter of the book summarizes its major conclusions and offers a brief outline of subsequent developments. A bibliography of relevant sources has been appended.

It is a pleasant task to acknowledge the generous assistance this work has received from many scholars and friends. Professor L. V. Thomas of Princeton University, under whose direction this study was originally carried out as a dissertation, Ph.D.(1957), offered numerous valuable suggestions concerning the methodology and organization of the work. Professors C. E. Dawn of the University of Illinois, Farhat Ziadeh and Morroe Berger, both of Princeton, and Dr. L. O. Schuman of the University of Amsterdam were all kind enough to read the original manuscript with great care and to offer detailed comments and criticisms which aided substantially in revising the work for publication. The perceptive counsel of my wife, given generously at all stages of preparing this book, contributed to its clarity and organization. For her efforts an expression of gratitude is hardly adequate.

The work also owes much to the knowledge and encouragement of two scholars who, though not involved directly in the manuscript, were indeed helpful to its author, namely Professor Emeritus Philip K. Hitti and Professor T. Cuyler Young, Chairman of the

Department of Oriental Studies at Princeton. An appointment as a Research Associate in the latter department during the 1961–1962 academic year made it possible for me to revise and expand the original manuscript to its present form. To all these individuals and to Princeton University I am indeed grateful, although they are to be absolved of responsibility for any errors or shortcomings which the reader may find.

Ibrahim Abu-Lughod
Northampton, Mass., 1962

INTRODUCTION

The Setting of Westernization

The history of the Arab world during the nineteenth and twentieth centuries is essentially the history of a transformation. A culture predominantly Muslim in orientation, belief, and commitment was being changed, suddenly and gradually, eagerly yet resisting, into a secular and westernized one. A society which had been living in a state of equilibrium within the protective framework of enviable isolation was suddenly exposed to the dynamic and less secure ground of the alien West, required to regain her balance and reorder her basic structure. This reorganization is still in process.

Several centuries of isolation, staticism, and decay had brought Islamic society to a nadir by the eighteenth century. Here was a society trying to subsist on its inner resources, but resources which by then had been drained and depleted, cut off as they were from their original well-spring by more than five centuries. The decline was general, encompassing almost every area of human activity. By the eighteenth century, the creative spark which had prompted earlier Arabs to explore and develop literature and the arts, science, philosophy, theology, jurisprudence, and geography was totally played out. In its place had been substituted formalization and pedanticism. In place of the tight if despotic control of a vast empire, the eighteenth century offered anarchic local regimes often only nominally responsible to the central administration in Istanbul. Finally, here was a society living in a resigned if not benign state of *Nirvana,* content with the small blessings of God, unquestioning of its lot, and blithely unconcerned with the bursting energy of a dynamic and expanding Europe.[1]

1. A portrayal of Islamic society prior to westernization can be found in H. A. R. Gibb and H. Bowen, *Islamic Society and the West, Vol. 1: Islamic Society in the*

Turkey, because of her close proximity to that bubbling cauldron of activity and because she had received several humiliating defeats at the hands of once subject or fearful neighbors, was keenly aware of Europe; she could not help but be. However, her more distant provinces were scarcely cognizant of these repeated defeats. The Arab provinces of the Middle East lived in the shadow of the Ottoman Empire which obscured from their view the dramatic shifts which were then taking place in the world's power structure.

That these shifts were inevitable is obvious when one contrasts the state of both societies at the time. On the one side was the West, where new advances in science and the technology of warfare were being applied with dramatic success. On the other was the Ottoman Empire, still defending itself with lances and outmoded cavalry tactics.[1]

On the one side was the West, where intellectual ferment was not only leavening the various branches of science but transforming the mechanical arts and recasting literature, philosophy, and political theory. On the other side were the Arabs and Turks, so entirely absorbed in refining prose and commenting on commentaries that, had a new thought occurred, it would have been voluntarily suppressed as a breach of etiquette.

At the very same time when the West was vigorously engaged in consolidating the European nation-state system and in encouraging the emergence of national loyalties and integrity, the Universal Ottoman Empire was gradually disintegrating. First it watched the dissolution of its European provinces; then it began to lose all but fiscal and nominal control over its Arab provinces. In the far south the Empire was threatened by a "fundamentalist" revolt which, while theologically motivated, was hardly devoid of political implications.

Eighteenth Century, in two parts, London: 1950 and 1957. For a summary of eighteenth-century Syria, see A. Hourani, "The Changing Face of the Fertile Crescent in the XVIIIth Century," *Studia Islamica*, Vol. viii, Paris: 1957, pp. 89–122. See also. J. Heyworth-Dunne, "Arabic Literature in Egypt in the 18th Century," in *Bulletin of the School of Oriental Studies*, Vol. ix, Part 3, London: 1938, pp. 675–689.

1. See Bernard Lewis, "Some Reflections on the Decline of the Ottoman Empire," *Studia Islamica*, Vol. ix, Paris: 1958, pp. iii-127, and his *The Emergence of Modern Turkey*, London: 1961, pp. 25–39.

This Wahhābi movement of the eighteenth century – and the inability of the Ottoman regime to bring it to a swift end – can be viewed as a serious symptom of decaying power. Another symptom was the impertinent independence of the local lords in Syria and Egypt, which augured ill for the Ottoman future. While it was still too early for national revolts, the general weakening of the Ottoman state was to be observed in sporadic rebellions and isolated but audacious acts. The Bedouins, never really disciplined or subdued, had nevertheless been circumscribed in their behavior at the height of Ottoman power. That they raided pilgrim caravans with increasing impunity is again merely indicative of the weakening central power.[1]

Citizens within the Ottoman Empire were feeling less secure and more oppressed as a result of blatant corruption, miscarriages of justice, and arbitrary rulings by government officials. Training of intelligent and disciplined public servants had suffered from the general decline in education, and their lack proved lethal to the development of a justice-oriented society. The corruption of these officials resulted, in the short run, in a general loss of confidence and, in the long run, in an almost complete shift in expectations. The officials were symbols of their system. As people lost confidence in the symbols they began also to question the system itself. Isolated individuals of the Ottoman Empire, particularly in the neglected Arab provinces, began to distrust the ruling institution, a distrust augmented by the growing insecurity of life and property. Contrast this, as Arabs were to do, with the fact that in Europe absolutism was waning and that constitutionalism and individualism were the new watch-words of that society.

One might dwell at length on the great differences between the two societies. This objective contrast, however, was sharpened still more by subjective perceptions. Not only were the societies different, but each was conscious of its apartness. Muslim Near East and Christian Europe were not only fundamentally opposed but each felt its own distinctness and each clothed its hostility in *noblesse oblige*.

Real differences in culture and religion cannot account entirely

1. Hourani, *op. cit.*, pp. 94–95.

for the alienation. It was due rather to a heritage deeply ingrained in each. The Arabs of the eighteenth century suffered from the legacy of their glorious past which had coincided with Europe's darkest age. That legacy made the isolated Arab of the eighteenth century feel a certain smugness toward all Europeans whom he judged as barbarians or, at best, somewhat dull and backward boors. His anachronistic attitude, based on an image formed earlier and transmitted from one generation to the next without benefit of new information, was that European society had nothing of worth to offer.[1]

Furthermore, the initial victories of the Ottomans still had the Arabs dazzled. The Turks had been successful and the Arabs of the Empire had shared in the reflected glory. That they were no longer powerful was an uncomfortable fact and was rejected or repressed. The implications of Ottoman defeat were eventually brought home to the Arabs, but *not* by the Turks.

The Europeans, represented by the army of a then-victorious Napoleon, appeared suddenly without warning or preparation at the most important center of the Arab provinces. The French expedition to Egypt in 1798 struck a crushing blow to the complacency of centuries, not just a humiliating one to the Mamlūk defenders. Here was a new image of the European; here was an enforced contact of cultures; but here also was a situation more baffling and perplexing than it was illuminating.

While the attempt to comprehend the newcomers and the culture they represented began slowly and was hindered throughout both by defenses and misjudgments, the process which was to steer Arab development westward had been set in motion. From that point onward, there began a shift in goals, actions, and even identification, until in the twentieth century a noted Egyptian humanist could claim that Egypt, and by extension all the Arab world, belonged to the larger western world.[2] Thus, from the hostile apartness perceived

1. Earlier Muslim and Arab awareness of the West is discussed by B. Lewis in his "The Muslim Discovery of the West," *Bulletin of the School of Oriental and African Studies*, Vol. xx, London: 1957, pp. 407–419.

2. Ṭāha Ḥusayn, *Mustaqbal al-Thaqāfah fi Miṣr*, Cairo: 1938, translated by Sidney Glazer, *The Future of Culture in Egypt*, Washington: 1954.

in the eighteenth century, there was a complete shift to the view that both societies, though at different levels and culturally unique, were *within the same framework.* This later sense of identity with the West plus the initial impulse toward change were set in motion by the French expedition.

The transformation which occurred during the little more than a century and a half of intensive contact which followed that event is both complex and fascinating. These years marked the passing of a "traditional" society and its metamorphosis into one with "modern" techniques, social and political institutions, and problems.[1] The process was not unique to the Arabs. Many other traditional societies, confronted by western cultural dominance, experienced similar transfigurations. All of these cases have similarities.[2] And yet each case, also, is unique. The similarities derive from the nature of the culture being transmitted. The disparities between results reflect the nature of the culture absorbing. But in order to understand the general phenomenon, there must be many case studies of particular aspects of westernization in particular societies.

Westernization,[3] however, is an extremely broad concept, including as it does a variety of aspects of culture and a variety of means whereby elements are transferred and adapted. This process may refer, for example, to the transformative effects of a new machine

1. Daniel Lerner, *The Passing of Traditional Society*, Glencoe: 1958.

2. For comparative purposes the reader is referred to J. K. Fairbank, "China's Response to the West: Problems and Suggestions," *Journal of World History*, Vol. III, Paris: 1956, pp. 381–406; and to J. Numata, "Acceptance and Rejection of Elements of European Culture in Japan," *Journal of World History*, Vol. III, Paris: 1956, pp. 231–251. Both of these articles analyze motivations which led to westernization and reactions to the process.

3. Despite the inadequacies of this term, it is perhaps the most accurate of all the terms used to describe the process of social and political change in the modern Middle East. It does not imply total transplantation of Western culture to an Arab environment, but merely that the stimuli for certain changes in Arab culture have their origins in the West. It implies no value judgment that these changes are in an inherently superior or "progressive" direction. It merely describes – for better or worse – the nature of the changes. Finally, it is somewhat broader in scope than some of the more limiting terms in circulation, such as "industrialization," which emphasize one aspect of culture while neglecting others. See D. A. Rustow, *Politics and Westernization in the Near East*, Princeton: 1956, pp. 4–6.

(an artifact), or a system of education (a social institution), or an idea (ideology) such as nationalism or constitutional government. It may refer in addition to the adoption and adaptation of the behavior patterns associated with such artifacts, institutions, and ideologies.

Not only are the "items" that are transmitted from one culture to another varied and complex but each transmitted item is differentially absorbed. In a few cases the new cultural phenomenon can be adopted freely, without danger of its coming into conflict with pre-existing patterns. More commonly, however, the new phenomenon may coexist uneasily for long periods of time with older, more indigenous cultural forms, the process of fusion and mutual modification taking place gradually.[1] Sometimes the new drives out the old only after the conflict has been spent. These variations make the task of assessing the impact of the new phenomenon infinitely more difficult.

When a cultural trait is being transmitted from one culture to another, the routes are often indirect. Many actors, or as we have termed them, "culture-carriers," may be involved, different ones at different stages of the transmission. Some are exogenous to the culture, foreigners who have direct contact with the native society. Some of these foreigners may unwittingly set an example which members of the indigenous society then attempt to emulate. Others may act more directly by introducing specific policies and institutions of foreign origin. Still others may influence, through education or other means, segments of the indigenous population who then translate what they have learned into specific changes in their own culture. Foreigners

---

1. Virtually no study of social change in the contemporary Arab world fails to emphasize this juxtaposition, in social and political life, of the older patterns and the newer imports from the West. Among the studies which have mentioned this are H. A. R. Gibb, "Social Change in the Near East," in P. Ireland, ed., *The Near East*, Chicago: 1942, pp. 33–67; Gibb, *Whither Islam*, London: 1932, pp. 315–379; A. Hourani, *Syria and Lebanon*, London: 1946, pp. 75–95; L. V. Thomas and R. Frye, *The United States and Turkey and Iran*, Cambridge: 1951, pp. 45–57; H. Kohn, *Western Civilization in the Near East*, London: 1936, pp. 87–114 and 227–305; D. A. Rustow, "The Politics of the Near East," in G. A. Almond and J. S. Coleman, *The Politics of the Developing Areas*, Princeton: 1960, pp. 369–452; M. Berger, *Bureaucracy and Society in Modern Egypt*, Princeton: 1957; A. J. Ahmed, *The Intellectual Origins of Egyptian Nationalism*, London: 1960.

undoubtedly played an important role in the process of westernization in the Arab world, but their action always required "local" interpreters in order to have an effect, which cannot be ignored when tracing the process.

This second set of actors consists of members of the indigenous society who in some way or another were changed by their contact with western culture. Some Arabs were influenced by their direct dealings with foreigners in their own country. Others were influenced by travel abroad, still others by an indirect contact with western culture derived from books. Regardless of the source of the influence, their role was a crucial one. They played it in two ways. First, some brought about changes in Arab society in a direct *de facto* manner, by introducing new administrative policies and programs. No less important were those whose effect was indirect. Arabs who wrote about the West tried to describe and interpret western culture and westerners for Arab readers who were otherwise denied such contact; in so doing, they helped to shape the concepts and attitudes of many of their fellow citizens. These actors must also be included in any study of the westernization of the Arab world.

Thus the complexity of the process of westernization arises from three contributing sources. First, western culture itself is complex, made up of a variety of aspects and dimensions not all of which enter another culture simultaneously or with equal impact. Second, Arab culture is also a complex but coherent system, so that even those aspects of the West which are transmitted to it do not meet with simultaneous acceptance and response. And third, the kinds of actors involved in the process of transmission are so varied in their nature and methods of influence that each must be studied independently.

To attempt to generalize about the westernization of the Arab world, given all these facets of the problem, would be premature. Even if the matter were less complex, there would not be adequate factual data to aid the task. Studies are lacking which trace, strand by strand, specific western concepts from their initial introduction to their final incorporation into Arab culture. Before more than tentative generalizations can be arrived at, a very large number of case studies must be made. This book attempts one such case study. From the complexity of cultural items transmitted, it focuses chiefly on certain basic political concepts which were introduced early into the Arab world. From the complexity of "responses," it focuses chiefly on the attitudes engendered, rather than on the specific programs into which these attitudes were incorporated. And, from the complexity of "actors" involved in the process of transmission, it selects chiefly those Arabs who, having gained a knowledge of western culture, transmitted their views to the Arab reading public in books published during the critical first seven decades of the nineteenth century when the seeds of westernization were first being planted.

ONE

Arab Awareness of the West: Modern Beginnings

The arrival of the French forces at Alexandria on the third of July, 1798, for the ostensible purpose of cutting off British communications with India, was as dramatic as it was consequential for the internal development of Arab society. It was a demonstration of European might which the Arab subjects of a decaying Ottoman-Mamlūk system could neither ignore nor comprehend. The initial victories of the French forces over the Mamlūk soldiers of Egypt demonstrated beyond any doubt the weakness of the once invincible Muslim armies. However, the French campaign assumes significance not from these military aspects but from the social and cultural forces engendered.

The French soldiers fought under the banner of the French Revolution. They represented a system diametrically opposed to many systems, including that of Ottoman Egypt. As individuals they may have had some effect on the population with whom they came in contact, but this is unlikely or at least conjectural. What is certain, however, is that their invasion smashed, once and for all, the isolating curtain which surrounded Egypt and the Fertile Crescent, marking the end of a long era.

The physical presence of French soldiers and auxiliary personnel was short lived, although a few of the latter remained to work for the successor state of Muḥammad 'Ali. By 1801, the army had been forced to retreat by a series of British-inflicted defeats on land and sea. During the occupation, however, the French instituted a number of administrative changes, some of which survived the withdrawal of their forces. In addition, during the three years of occupation, soldiers and savants transacted business with the native population and came into limited contact with certain subgroups of that population in the joint efforts to administer the country. Such contacts must have evoked a reaction of some sort, must have piqued the curiosity of individual Arabs. Yet the historian of culture-contact, attempting to assess the significance of such interaction, is faced with a total absence of any literary work describing even meagerly the nature and impact of such contacts. In the absence of such documents, all conclusions concerning this matter are merely inferential.

Our concern, however, is with more concrete questions. What ideas were transmitted at this early period and what kind of image of the French did the Arabs form on the basis of this abortive contact?

Those familiar with the French campaigns in Egypt are aware of the edicts and proclamations which Napoleon, as Commander of the Army, issued for the benefit of the Egyptian population. Apart from the sincerity of such proclamations, they were an important vehicle through which a number of European ideas and concepts were introduced. They constitute the first channel through which these European ideas entered the Arab world. Nor did impact stop at their issuance. The incomprehensibility of the ideas impelled a number of contemporary Arab chroniclers to explain and discuss them at some length. In addition, they found it necessary to provide the Arab reading public with some background information about the mysterious French and about their history. Thus we must consider not only the proclamations themselves but also the interpretations and commentaries they stimulated.

The Napoleonic Proclamations

During the course of the French campaign and occupation, a large number and variety of edicts and proclamations were issued, many of which dealt specifically with the mechanics of occupation. None of the later proclamations seems to have had as important an effect in transmitting ideas as the very first Napoleonic edict written aboard his ship, the *Orient,* one day prior to the actual invasion of Egypt. This proclamation was translated into Arabic by the orientalists attached to the expedition and printed in that language for subsequent distribution in Alexandria and Cairo. Later Napoleonic proclamations were to reiterate single principles taken from this first prototype or to deal exclusively with daily requirements of the French forces. The Proclamation stated:[1]

> In the name of God, the Merciful and Compassionate; there is no God but God;
>
> In the name of the French Republic [*Jumhūr*], based upon the foundations of Liberty and Equality, Bonaparte, the Commander-in-Chief of the French Forces, informs all the population of Egypt:
>
> For a long time, those in power in Egypt have insulted the French Nation [*Millah*] and unfairly treated her merchants by various deceitful and aggressive tactics. Now, the hour of their punishment has arrived.
>
> For many decades, these Mamlūks, who were brought in from the Caucasus and Georgia, have been corrupting the best region of the whole world. But God, the Omnipotent, the Master of the Universe, has now made the destruction of their state imperative.

1. The original Arabic version is no longer extant. We have relied in this translation on the versions conserved in the Arab chronicles of the French expedition. The few discrepancies which occur in the several versions are noted in our analysis. Similarly, discrepancies between French and Arabic versions are noted, wherever they occur. Specifically, the English translation given above is from the version of Niqūla al-Turk, *Mudhakkirāt*, edited and translated into French by Gaston Wiet, *Nicolas Turc, Chronique d'Egypte* 1798–1804, Cairo: 1950, pp. 8–11.

As will be observed later in the text, Jabarti's version is slightly different, particularly in the Preamble. However, the text of the communiqué is substantially the same in all the Arabic documents examined. See, for other versions, 'Abd al-Raḥmān al-Jabarti, *'Ajā'ib al-āthār fi al-Tarājim wa al-Akhbār*, Vol. III, Cairo: 1879, pp. 4–5. (French translation by Chefik Mansour *et al., Merveilles biographiques et historiques du Cheikh Abd el-Rahman el-Jabarti*, Tome vi, Cairo: 1892, pp. 10–12.) See also David Ayalon, "The Historian al-Jabarti and his Background," in BSOAS, Vol. xxiii, Part 2, London: 1960, pp. 217–249; and Ḥaydar A. al-Shihābi, *Lubnān fi 'Ahd al-Umarā' al-Shihābīyīn*, (Lebanon during the Shihabis), edited by A. Rustum and F. al-Bustāni, Beirut: 1933, pp. 222–224.

There are slight differences between the Arabic translations and the French original. The first paragraph of the Arabic Preamble has no French counterpart. See H. Plon and J. Dumaine, eds., *Correspondances de Napoléon Ier*, Vol. IV, Paris: 1860, Communiqué No. 2723, 2 July 1798, pp. 191–192. See also Christian Cherfils, *Bonaparte et l'Islam*, Paris: 1914, for reprints of other French proclamations.

People of Egypt, some may say to you that I did not come except to obliterate your religion. That is an outright lie; do not believe it. Tell those fabricators that I came only to rescue your rights from the oppressors. And that I worship Almighty God, and respect his Prophet Muḥammad and the glorious *Qur'ān* more than the Mamlūks do. Tell them also that all people are equal before God.

The only grounds for distinctions among them are reason, virtue, and knowledge. [But] what virtue, reason, and knowledge distinguish the Mamlūks from others which would give them exclusive rights over everything that makes life sweet? Wherever there is fertile land, it belongs to the Mamlūks; so also do they exclusively possess the most beautiful maids, horses, and houses.

If the Egyptian land has been bestowed on them, let them produce the Title which God wrote for them. But God, the Master of the Universe, is compassionate and just with his people. With God's help, from now on, no Egyptian will be barred from entering the highest positions [of the State] and from acquiring the most elevated status. The intelligent, virtuous and learned men will take charge of affairs and thus the plight of the entire nation will improve.[1]

Formerly, there were great cities, wide canals, and thriving commerce in Egypt, all of which have disappeared as a result of the Mamlūks' greed and oppression.

Judges, Shaykhs, Imāms, officers and notables of the country, inform your people that the French are also faithful Muslims.[2] As proof of this, they attacked Great Rome, where they destroyed the Papal Throne, which was always urging the Christians to fight the Muslims. Then they went to Malta from which they expelled the Knights who allege that Almighty God asked them to fight the Muslims. In addition, the French at every time have been the most faithful friends of the Ottoman Sultan and the enemy of his enemies, may God preserve his reign[3] and destroy the Mamlūks who refused to obey him and heed his orders. They [Mamlūks] only obeyed him originally to advance their personal greed.

1. According to the French original, this sentence should have been rendered: "All Egyptians are called upon to manage all posts; the wisest, the most learned, and the most virtuous shall govern, and the people shall be happy." Plon and Dumaine, *op cit.*, p. 191.

2. According to the French original, this phrase should have been rendered: "We have been true friends of the Muslims."

3. In the French original, this reads: "Have we not throughout the ages been unwavering friends of the Ottoman Sultan; May God preserve his reign."

Blessings and happiness to the Egyptian people who agree with us promptly, thus improving their own conditions and elevating their status. Happiness also to those who remain at home, taking no side in the fighting; they will hasten to our side when they know us better.

But woe to those who join the Mamlūks and aid them in the war against us; they will find no way to escape and no trace of them will be left.

ARTICLE I
All villages situated within a three-hour circumference of the areas through which the French Forces pass must send delegates to the commander of the troops, informing him of their obedience to the French Forces and that they have raised the tri-color flag.

ARTICLE II
Any village which takes up arms against the French Forces will be burned.

ARTICLE III
Any village which obeys the French Forces will also raise the flag of our friend, the Ottoman Sultan, may God prolong his existence.

ARTICLE IV
The shaykhs in each village will put under seal immediately the houses and properties of all those who collaborate with the Mamlūks. They should be extremely diligent so that no losses occur.

ARTICLE V
All the shaykhs, scholars, jurists and imāms [the functionaries of the state, that is] must continue their duties. Each inhabitant must remain safely at home. Also, all prayers will be conducted as usual in the Mosque. All Egyptians should be grateful to God for the destruction of the Mamlūks, praying aloud "May God conserve the glory of the Ottoman Sultan! May God preserve the glory of the French Forces! God's curse on the Mamlūks! May God improve the condition of the Egyptian Nation (*al-Ummah al-Miṣrīyah*)."
Written in the Headquarters at Alexandria, the 13th of Messidor

of the Sixth year of the French Republic [First of July, 1798], that is, the end of Muḥarram 1213 Higrī [18th of Muḥarram].[1]

This was the proclamation rendered into Arabic by the orientalists attached to the French expedition and left to us in its Arabic version in the three major works of Jabarti, al-Turk, and al-Shihābi. The proclamation conveyed information of two kinds. First, it presented, albeit in somewhat vague terms, information about the occupying forces – who they were, where they came from, and what they represented. Second, it introduced certain principles of political philosophy which were enunciated for the benefit of the Egyptian public. Our analysis of the communiqué is guided by these divisions.

In the proclamation, Napoleon informed the Egyptians that he and his forces were Frenchmen and that they represented the French Republic, which was based upon liberty and equality. Thus, an attempt was made to introduce the concept of "Republic" to an Arab audience for the first time. The word used by Napoleon's orientalist interpreters to convey the concept of Republic was *jumhūr*, the literal meaning of which is simply "Public." Since no parallel concept existed in Arabic at that time, this was merely an attempt to approximate the western concept, which later came to be rendered more accurately in Arabic as *jumhūrīyah*.[2]

---

1. Actually, the original date of the communiqué was the 14th of Messidor (the 2nd of July), and the place was on the ship of Napoleon.

2. Bernard Lewis, in his article "The Concept of an Islamic Republic," *Die Welt Des Islam*, Vol. IV, Leiden: 1955, pp. 1–3, states that: "This word [jumhūrīyah] is an innovation of the late nineteenth century. The need for a word to express the notion 'Republic' was felt rather earlier, in 1798, when the French expedition under Napoleon came to Egypt and began to issue proclamations and edicts in Arabic in the name of the French Republic. The word used by the translators attached to the French expedition was *Mashyakha*, an Arabic noun which is derived from the well-known word sheikh ... "

Professor Lewis added that the Turks were familiar with the concept *jumhūr* through their dealings with the Republic of Venice but preferred not to use the term. According to Lewis: "This word *jumhūr* took on new life after the French Revolution, when it was used in Turkish documents to describe the French Republic, as well as other republics ... As late as the 1870's the word *jumhūr* was used in both Turkish and Arabic for republic, but in a very loose way, without any clear distinction being made between the two meanings of public and republic. Writers wishing to discuss the republic as a form of government were still forced to use cumbersome and

Another concept introduced by the Napoleonic communiqué reactivated an older principle which had long been dormant in the Islamic milieu. In the communiqué, Napoleon justified his attack on Egypt not only in terms of the maltreatment of French merchants but also on the claim that the Mamlūks were usurpers who were unjustly oppressing the majority of the people who differed from them ethnically. Napoleon communicated this principle by consistently drawing a line between the rulers, i.e. the Mamlūks, and the ruled, i.e. the Egyptians. Not only were the Mamlūks usurpers with no God-given right to rule Egypt but they had also unjustly monopolized the positions of the state. Napoleon argued implicitly that the Egyptians owed no loyalty to their rulers. Egyptian loyalty to Islam did not necessarily require subordination to their Mamlūk rulers or, for that matter, to any Muslim government that mistreated them in such fashion.

A third important political principle introduced by Napoleon – one which was not unknown to the Arabs but which had been so violated by Muslim governments in general and by the Mamlūks in

roundabout expressions ... The modern word *jumhūriyat* – which is simply *jumhūr* with an abstract ending – ... first appears in Turkey. From Turkey it spread eastwards to the Arabs, Persians and other peoples of Islam ... In its first appearance in the Turkish dictionary it is defined as 'the principle of government by the public – the mass.' Only towards the end of the nineteenth century does the word come to mean republic as well as – and then instead of – republicanism."

On the basis of evidence presented here, these remarks by Lewis, while accurately pointing to a basic problem of terminology, must be modified somewhat. First, Napoleon's translators did use the term *jumhūr* to stand for Republic in the original communiqué. The term *mashyakhah*, as will be shown in the following pages, was used exclusively by the Arabs themselves to convey in terms more meaningful to them the political meaning of Republic.

Second, and this also will be substantiated in a later section of this book, the word *jumhūrīyah* was used by Arab writers long before the "late 1870's" that Professor Lewis dates the term from. Rifā'ah R. Ṭahṭāwi used the term in 1834 to describe the form of government established in France at the abolition of the monarchy and, in fact, defined its meaning for his readers. See his *Takhlīṣ al-Ibrīz ila Talkhīṣ Bārīz*, first published in 1834. The edition used here was the third edition, published in Cairo in 1905, see pp. 79–81. Later translators of European text books on history, in works published in 1841 and 1847, used the word *jumhūrīyah*, and explained its meaning as republic in only brief discussions. See later p. 65. By 1867 the term was in fairly wide circulation, since Khayr al-Dīn Pāsha al-Tūnisi used it in his book without giving any definition or explanation for the meaning. (See pp. 108 and 111 below.)

particular that its reaffirmation was novel – was the concept of the right of all people to equal opportunity. In contrast to the prevailing attitude of resignation to the caste-like system of social status under the Mamlūks, Napoleon emphasized the right of anyone to occupy the position to which his abilities and qualifications entitled him. Related to this was the tentative promise made in the communiqué that a native Egyptian government would be established to run the affairs of the country. Even the fact that no such government was ever set up does not detract from the importance of such a principle. No other conqueror of Egypt had ever suggested such a policy.

One final element in the communiqué should also be mentioned, even though it had no immediate impact. This was a distinct appeal to the concepts of Egyptian nationalism and of an Egyptian Nation (*al-Ummah al-Miṣrīyah*).

A few of the omissions of the communiqué may also be significant. For example, one notes that the word "fraternity" is omitted from its traditional place in the trilogy of "liberty, equality, and fraternity."[1] It is difficult to explain this omission, especially in the light of the stress placed on the basic fraternity between the French and Muslim peoples. Napoleon argued that he worshipped the same God and respected the Prophet and the *Qur'ān,* and, further, he cited the permanent alliance between the Ottoman government and the French as evidence of his championship of the Muslim cause. On the other hand, he claimed that his enmity for the Muscovites was motivated by a desire to protect the Ottoman Empire as well as by French abhorrence of the "corrupt" and "polytheistic" trinitarians of Russia.[2]

These were the salient aspects of the Napoleonic communiqué. Subsequent proclamations were to reiterate the concept of the republic and the symbols of the French Revolution often enough, but no major additions were made in terms of political concepts.

These ideas – republic, ethnic composition of the state, social equality and mobility, and the "just" state – were expressed in the

1. See the suggestive remarks of B. Lewis, *The Emergence of Modern Turkey*, London: 1961, p. 54.

2. See al-Turk, *op. cit.*, pp. 55–56; Shihābi, *op. cit.*, pp. 214–215, 230–235, 269–272, 275–276, 278–279.

proclamation and offered as representing the belief system of the invading Europeans. Though destined to be of major importance in later Arab developments, these concepts seem to have produced no immediate effect whatsoever. While the expressions of such radical beliefs were causing major revolutions and rebellions in Europe, they fell on deaf ears at the beginning of the nineteenth century in Egypt.

That they had no immediate effect upon Arab society, may be related to the fact that these ideas were insufficiently understood by the masses and even by the cultural spokesmen of the time. It is obvious that the adoption of an idea depends in part upon comprehension and is in large measure influenced by the status of the group through which it is introduced. Therefore, the proclamations cannot be judged in a vacuum; they must be judged within the context of their introduction. It is to the interpretations of the contemporary Arab historians that we must turn now, since their reactions to the proclamations constitute the first aspect of modern Arab awareness of the West.

The Arab Chroniclers of the French Expedition

The history of the French expedition to Egypt is recorded in the works of three Arab chroniclers of the early nineteenth century: the Egyptian, ʿAbd al-Raḥmān al-Jabarti (d. 1825); the Syrian, Niqūla al-Turk (d. 1828); and the Lebanese, Haydar al-Shihābi (d. 1835). Their accounts represent the highest degree of articulate awareness of the West that the Arab world had reached by that particular time, at least in written form.

JABARTI'S ACCOUNT

Jabarti begins his narration by informing his readers of the arrival of British ships in Alexandria harbor in search of French vessels. Finding none, they soon set sail again. Shortly thereafter the French arrived, disembarked at Alexandria, and began their march on Cairo. In both cities the French distributed the first Napoleonic Proclamation. Jabarti's rendition of the Proclamation was complete, except for one extremely significant omission: he deleted the word "Republic" from the preamble. His version reads "on behalf of the

French" instead of "on behalf of the French Republic."[1] Not only did he omit this perplexing term from his edition of the communiqué but even after he had gained knowledge of the background of Napoleon he still preferred to ignore it. In paraphrasing official French documents, he simply dismisses the term and its connotation. Thus we find one of the most important concepts of the French Revolution eluding one of the best spokesmen of the Arab world at the time.

That Jabarti failed to comprehend the term is perhaps symptomatic of something deeper than strangeness. Had Arabs of the time been at all interested in Europe and the course of European events, they could not but help having heard something of the revolutionary movement sweeping that continent. Evidently, their ignorance was almost total. What little they knew through hearsay was without consequence. This is further confirmed by an ignorance of France. We look in vain for information about the occupying forces, their origin, and their motives in coming to Egypt. That they were "French" is abundantly clear. That they were in some way in conflict with the "British" is also established. But why had they come to Egypt at all? Did they go elsewhere? Who were they? These questions are ignored.

Only fragmentary information is available in the historical account of Jabarti. Besides being French and Christian, we are told, the invaders "founded" their state about the year 1792, as evidenced by the fact that they celebrated with great pomp and extravagance the anniversary of their Republic (*Qiyām al-Jumhūr bi Bilādihim*) in an all-night feast in the Gardens of Ezbekīyah in Cairo. Beyond that, Jabarti would not commit himself.[2]

Although Jabarti thus neglects both the concept of the Republic and the historic development of France, he does present an image of the French which is of great interest because it was to be reinforced by subsequent observers. In the course of narrating the activities of the

1. Jabarti, *op. cit.*, pp. 4 and 116–134.

2. *Ibid.*, pp. 16–18 and pp. 81–82 for a description of a later celebration. It is interesting to point out that in the course of Jabarti's description of the first festival he notes that their priest (*Kabīr Qusūsihim*) delivered a sermon to the assembled soldiers. Apparently, the anti-religious bias of the French Revolution and its secular nature were hardly recognized by Jabarti. See below, p. 140.

French, Jabarti describes a French intellectual establishment (*Institut d'Egypte*), where the French installed their scholars and housed an excellent library with a wide variety of books, including those written in Arabic and other Islamic languages. He seems to have been deeply impressed with the abundance of scientists attached to that establishment, fascinated by their strange equipment and their occasional experiments. These aroused the curiosity of the Egyptian historian. Furthermore, he observed with approbation their serious method of work, their courtesy to curious visitors of the native population, and their interest in "educating" intelligent Egyptians who frequented the *Institut*. This side of the French he not only appreciated but on occasion used to his own advantage.[1]

This was the favorable side of the image of the once-despised culture. Yet there was another, less complimentary one. The historian also took a look at a different segment of French personnel: the soldiers. What he saw merely reinforced or confirmed existing stereotypes. For in the markets of Cairo he was a witness to more than one drunken brawl. The French, he concluded, were unfortunately habitual drunkards, fond of frivolities, and dedicated to the search of pleasure.[2]

How can Jabarti's contribution be summarized? First, he remained unimpressed by the victory of the French over the local Mamlūk lords, since it implied to him no necessary superiority. Second, he tended to ignore, either from lack of interest or because of their unfamiliar quality, French political concepts of state and society. Third, he demonstrated an ambivalent reaction to the Frenchmen with whom he came in contact, admiring the dedicated scholars of the *Institut* while condemning the remainder as decadent and ill-mannered.

NIQŪLA AL-TURK'S TREATMENT

The entire diaries of Niqūla al-Turk are concerned with the French occupation of Egypt and Syria. His understanding of the French and

---

1. *Ibid.*, pp. 34–35. This impression was to be reinforced as awareness of the West increased. See later chapters.
2. *Ibid.*, pp. 44 and 51.

their background, which is incorporated in the introduction to his diaries, goes a substantial distance beyond that of Jabarti.

In his introduction, al-Turk notes that in order to understand the French occupation one must consider events taking place on the continent of Europe, for the occupation was but an extension of a long series of events originating elsewhere. Within this framework he set for himself the task of describing "the circumstances surrounding the rise of the French Republic (*Mashyakhah*) which not only resulted in the death of the French monarch but inspired numerous seditions in the various Frankish lands. Although it suffered several reverses initially, the French Republic finally established a prominent influence in Europe by virtue of the military victories achieved by the courageous and indefatigable General Bonaparte."

According to his narration:[1]

> The people of France in this year (1792) arose in total upheaval … against the King, the princes, and the nobility, demanding a new constitution and a modern order in place of the existing regime … claiming … that the absolute power of the King had inflicted great damage on the Kingdom … and that the princes and nobility enjoyed the wealth of the country while the rest of the people lived in abject poverty and submission. For this reason they all arose with a united voice, saying 'there shall be no comfort for us unless the King abdicates and the Republic (*mashyakhah*) is established … no longer should the King be free to render a judgment or publish an opinion on his own counsel, but the conduct of affairs and the administration of the *monarchy* should depend upon the opinions of Senators (*mashāyyekh*) of the people, convened in an assembly where the *King has the first voice*, with *the Senators coming next.* By these means the state of the *Kingdom* would improve.' After listening to their demands, the King informed them that he too was similarly concerned with the progress and welfare of the realm and would, therefore, submit to their desires. Thereupon, they requested him to sign a convention which embodied their demands. The convention

1. This translation has been made from the original Arabic version, *op. cit.*, pp. 2–4. In the French translation these quotations appear on pp. 3–5. Italics have been added here.

> included conditions for establishing a Republic (*mashyakhah*) and for *abolishing the absolute* power of the King.

In brief but ornamental prose al-Turk then details the ensuing violence, the anti-religious actions of the revolutionaries and ultimately the successive revolutionary wars. It was his opinion that these wars were caused not by the French but by the other European powers whose monarchs, fearful that their own subjects might be influenced by the incendiary slogans of the revolution, sought to quell the source of the conflagration. The final outcome of these wars was a French victory and the invasion of Egypt to thwart British counterambitions.

The portrayal by al-Turk, however, is far from lucid. The many concepts which inspired the French Revolution are given no coherent treatment. The form of government espoused by the revolutionists was evidently unclear to him. Thus, rather than deal with the perplexing concept of a republic, he preferred to transform it into a more familiar institution, the *mashyakhah* (council of the elders), the existence of which was not incompatible with a limited monarchy. It is significant; in this context, to point out that, although al-Turk reproduced the first Napoleonic Proclamation with the word *Jumhūr* (Republic) intact, in his own paraphrasing of the meaning of the proclamation, he reverted to the use of the more familiar term, *mashyakhah*.

The work of al-Turk is significant in two major ways. In the first place, it represents the first exposition in Arabic of contemporary European events and constitutes the first true "reaction" to the French Revolution in the Arab world. In the second place, it constituted the basic reference upon which later historians of the period were to build their accounts.

THE CHRONICLER, HAYDAR AL-SHIHĀBI

The Lebanese historian Haydar al-Shihābi relied heavily on the work of al-Turk for his background data on the French and their revolution. He also chronicled the French Revolution beginning with 1792 and discussed in almost identical phrases the people's demand for a constitution and a modern regime. He recounted the same hypothetical conversation between the insurgents and the King, the outcome of which was the King's signing of the convention which embodied conditions "to suit the reform of the Kingdom and the establishment of a Republic (*mashyakhah*)."[1] The revolutionary wars and the subsequent victories of France were treated with admiration. Shihābi, while following closely the prior treatment by al-Turk, did augment the account by including his translation of a Turkish work dealing with Napoleon's campaigns on the continent.[2]

Of the other results of the French Revolution, little was noted, beyond the fact that there was a change in the French calendar and "other things that changed the old ways."[3] With obvious sympathy and regret, Shihābi, as well as al-Turk, recounted how the anti-religious campaigns resulted in the desecration and pillaging of churches, and how the monarch Louis XVI was apprehended in flight and cruelly beheaded. Their sympathies were all on the side of the monarch whom they admired for his courage in facing his "murderers."[4]

We might note also that the gradually rising tempo of the revolution was simply ignored by the chroniclers. Their dating the revolution from the year 1792 followed the French observance, but it implies perhaps in addition that they were unaware of or unable to sort out the turmoil of the years which preceded. The successive forms of organization and reorganization, from the *Constituante* (1789–1791) through the *Empire* (1804–1815), through which French revolutionary government passed are totally omitted from the chronicles. Only in passing is the reader

1. Shihābi, *op. cit.*, pp. 213–214.
2. *Ibid.*, pp. 441–524.
3. *Ibid.*, pp. 218–219.
4. al-Turk, *op. cit.*, pp. 1–6; Shihābi, *op. cit.*, pp. 214–221. Interestingly enough, both chroniclers reproduced the final speech which Louis XVI was alleged to have delivered prior to his execution. See the earlier edition of al-Turk's version in M. Desgranges, *Histoire de l'expédition des Français en Egypte*, Paris: 1839, pp. 5–10. See also Ra'īf Khūri, *Al-Fikr al-'Arabi al-Ḥadīth* (Modern Arab Thought) Beirut: 1943, pp. 91–92.

informed that Napoleon's title had changed from *Qunṣul* (Consul) to *Imbarāṭūr* (Emperor).[1] How, why, and when this change took place is nowhere to be found.

The reaction of the chroniclers to the revolution is best characterized as ambivalent. The most impressive positive contribution of the revolution, insofar as the chroniclers were concerned, seems to have been the military victories to which it led. Glowing adjectives modify references to military successes. The revolution itself received far less approbation. It is described always in demeaning terms such as *balbalah* (hubbub) and *fitnah* (sedition), revealing an essential repugnance on the part of the authors. While it is true that the revolution was inextricably related in their minds to the subsequent emergence of Napoleon, whom they seem to have admired personally, the violence of the revolution and particularly its anti-religious tone evoked condemnation.[2] Finally, in their acknowledgement of French unity under revolutionary principles, there was the beginning of an awareness of nationalism as a new basis of unity.

The three impressions of the French Revolution, although far from sharply delineated and lucidly expounded, together with Jabarti's direct impressions of Frenchmen on the scene, were destined to become more significant in later developments of nineteenth-century Arab society.[3] Until the time of Muḥammad 'Ali,

1. Shihābi, *op. cit.*, pp. 441 ff.
2. See later, pp. 130–134.
3. It has been suggested that information about the French Revolution had an early and important impact on nineteenth-century internal developments in Lebanon. This hypothesis is based primarily on evidence of terminology. According to two primary sources, rebellious Lebanese villages in 1820–1821 and 1840 made use of the terms *Jumhūr, Ḥukūmah Jumhūrīyah* (Republican Government), and *'Āmmīyah* (Commune), For this argument, see R. Khūri, *op. cit.*, pp. 89–94; and Philip K. Hitti, "The Impact of the west on Syria and Lebanon in the Nineteenth Century," *The Journal of World History*, Vol. II, No. 3, Paris: 1955, pp. 629–630. For the original sources from which these interpretations have been made, see Filīb and Farīd al-Khāzin, *Majmū'at al-Muḥarrarāt al-Siyāsīyah* (Collected Political Documents), Jūniyah: 1910–1911, pp. 384–385; and Anṭūn Ḍ. al-'Aqīqi, *Thawrah wa Fitnah fi Lubnān*, Beirut: 1936, pp. 87–90, translated by M. Kerr, *Revolution and Sedition in Lebanon*, Beirut: 1959, pp. 53–54.

they summed up Arab awareness of the West, an awareness which was, under that new ruler of Egypt, to expand in scope and deepen in dimension.

TWO

The Development of the Translation Movement

Just as the French expedition can be considered the first *stimulus* to modern Arab awareness of the West, so the activities undertaken by Muḥammad 'Ali Pasha during the first half of the nineteenth century can be viewed as the first Egyptian *response* to that awareness. Most historians date the true beginnings of westernization from that crucial era.

In their attempt to westernize, the Arabs of the nineteenth century chose a mode of transmitting western ideas and techniques which had been successfully exploited by their ninth-century ancestors – namely, the translation of western books into Arabic. But, since the new age was one dominated by utilitarian motives, the selection of books to be translated was governed by immediate necessity rather than discursive interest. The translated books were to be used in conjunction with a radically new system of education, one having only remote connection with the traditional pattern. In order to visualize this, we might state the problem in the following fashion: a culture trying to westernize introduces new subjects of instruction which it believes will bring about the desired changes, since the traditional curriculum is considered incapable of meeting the problems of change. However, the new subjects require both teaching personnel and books. Since neither is available, they are imported. Both must be able to communicate in the native language; accordingly, translation assumes central importance during this early stage.

This necessity, coupled with the attempt of Arabs of the nineteenth century to meet it, opened up a new channel whereby Arab awareness of the West was to spread. The translated material conveyed to an Arabic reading public substantive information about western society, as explained and interpreted by Europeans.

Obviously, this method of cultural exchange has equally significant advantages and disadvantages. If wisely selected, the translated material is capable of offering an authentic, sensitive, and sophisticated portrayal of western developments. If capriciously selected, it may seriously distort the image of the West. Thus, in studying the transmission of western ideas to the nineteenth-century Arab world, both the way in which western books were selected for translation and the nature of the books themselves must be taken into account. This chapter will trace the development of the translation movement from 1800 to 1870, focusing primarily upon the auspices under which translations were made and upon the criteria of selection. The substance of the translated material will be reserved to a succeeding chapter.

During the first half of the nineteenth century, the translation movement was almost entirely confined to activities supported, inspired, and organized by official quarters, chiefly Egyptian. The bulk of translated material at this time was the product of an official policy of the Egyptian state. Insofar as can be determined, no significant translation was undertaken outside official channels.

Beginning in the 1850s, this publicly sponsored movement was supplemented by less organized private activities. By that time educated individuals began to translate western books on their own initiative and their translations were published without official support. Most, although certainly not all, of the translations prepared under independent auspices during this later period originated in the Fertile Crescent rather than in Egypt. The independent translators were Arabs who had established contact with American and French missionaries who also did some translation. This later development in the translation movement was still in its early stages between 1850 and 1870. It reached fruition somewhat later, aided particularly by the younger intellectuals who had completed their studies at the recently established western institutions in Beirut, namely the Syrian Protestant College and the University of St. Joseph.

The earlier period of officially inspired and supported translation can be classified into five divisions, corresponding to changes in the official Egyptian policy governing the translation of western books into Arabic. These are:

1. Unorganized official interpreting, up to 1826
2. Random translations, between 1826 and 1835
3. Organized period of translation, 1835 to 1848
4. Decline of official translating, 1848 to 1863
5. Revival of the translation movement, 1863 upward.[1]

The Period of Unorganized Official Interpreting

The translating that was done during roughly the first quarter of the nineteenth century is more properly termed interpreting. Rather than being directed toward major European works, the bulk of the translating was official interpreting between the Egyptian state on the one hand and the foreign powers, represented by their consular officials, on the other hand.

In addition to the translation of communications between governmental representatives, a second type of "interpreting" was undertaken in 1816. In that year an Egyptian School of Engineering was established by Muḥammad 'Ali and staffed by a faculty of European instructors. Since these teachers were rarely able to lecture in Arabic, there was a pressing need for consecutive translation. The precedent for this procedure had already been established one year previously in the Military School founded by Muḥammad 'Ali in 1815.[2]

---

1. A somewhat modified approach to this organization is followed by Jāk Tājir in his *Ḥarakat al-Tarjamah bi Miṣr* (The Translation Movement in Egypt), Cairo: 1945, pp. 1–2. See also Jamāl al-Din al-Shayyāl, *Ta'rīkh al-Tarjamah wa al-Harakah al-Thaqāfiyah fi 'Aṣr Muḥammad 'Ali* (History of the Translation and Literary Movement in the Age of Muḥammad 'Ali), Cairo: 1951; and J. Heyworth-Dunne, "Printing and Translations under Muḥammad 'Ali of Egypt: the Foundation of Modern Arabic," in the *Journal of the Royal Asiatic Society*, London: 1940, pp. 325–349.
2. Tājir, *op. cit.*, pp. 15–24; see also J. Heyworth-Dunne, *An Introduction to the History of Education in Modern Egypt*, London: 1939, pp. 106–111.

The identity of the interpreters of this period cannot be established with certainty. Some of them, especially those who undertook official interpreting between the Egyptian state and the representatives of foreign European powers, were Europeans who had originally come to Egypt with the French military expedition in 1798 and elected to remain after that expedition departed in 1801. For the most part, they confined their translations to official documents and correspondence. Some of these translators did use their knowledge of Arabic to translate a few Arabic literary works into French, but they rendered no significant French books into Arabic.

The second group of translators, engaged chiefly in interpreting the lectures of European instructors in the schools of military science and engineering, was somewhat more heterogeneous. From the little that can be determined concerning them, they appear to have been Turks and Arabs who had managed somehow to master at least the rudiments of the foreign tongue.[1]

The significance of this early period of the translation movement is more symbolic than substantive. Its importance lies in the fact that at least a provisional measure of contact between the two cultures had been established and that, with this contact, there had developed an awareness of the need for communication. Translation was accepted as a technique for such communication but was still used in a narrow expediential manner during this earliest period.

The Period of Random Translation, 1826–1835

The need for translators was felt with increasing intensity as Muḥammad ʻAli launched his comprehensive program for education. From 1826 onward, the development of the translation movement went hand in hand with developments in the educational system of Egypt. In view of the close relationship between these two elements in the building of the new Egyptian state, it is necessary to dwell at least briefly on the schools established and on some of the problems involved in their operation.

---

1. Tājir, *op. cit.*, pp. 3–14; Shayyāl, *op. cit.*, pp. 16–36.

Muḥammad 'Ali hoped to create a stable, strong, and viable state in Egypt, patterned on the western European model.[1] To this end he founded a number of new institutions. Most of these institutions were geared toward the military machine of Muḥammad 'Ali, but an important by-product was the subsequent emergence of men and institutions whose functions in society far transcended the limits of military organization and efficiency. Among the non-military schools established by Muḥammad 'Ali were: the School of Engineering, established in 1816 and later transferred to and expanded in Būlāq in 1834; the School of Medicine, founded in 1827; the School of Pharmaceutics, 1829; the School of Mineralogy, 1834; the School of Agriculture, 1836; and the School of Translation, 1836. This school was later expanded in function and its name changed to correspond to the new functions assigned to it. Thus in 1841 it became known as the School of Languages and Accountancy; in 1868 it was identified as the School of Languages, Administration and Accountancy. In 1875 it became the School of Law and Administration.[2]

Implicit in this brief enumeration are a number of very basic facts. Perhaps the most important is that these schools were the first of their kind to be established in the Arab world in modern times. Therefore, they set the rudimentary pattern for a new educational system which eventually broke away completely from the traditional pattern of learning.[3]

---

1. For some brief accounts of this, see *The Cambridge Modern History*, Vol. x, New York: 1907, pp. 545–572; G. Young, *Egypt*, New York: 1927, pp. 23–62; M. Sabry, *L'Empire Egyptien sous Mohamed Ali et la question d'Orient*, Paris: 1930, pp. 579–592; H. Dodwell, *The Founder of Modern Egypt; A Study of Muhammad Ali,* Cambridge: 1931, pp. 192–241; N. Izzedin, *The Arab World*, Chicago: 1953, pp. 64–74; G. Kirk, *A Short History of the Middle East*, London: 1955, pp. 98–103; S. N. Fisher, *The Middle East*, London: 1960, pp. 277–286.
2. Amīn Sāmi, *al-Ta'līm fi Miṣr* (Education in Egypt), Cairo: 1917, pp. 13–34; A. 'Abd al-Karīm, *Ta'rīkh al-Ta'līm fi'Aṣr Muḥammad 'Ali* (History of Education in the Age of Muḥammad 'Ali), Cairo: 1938, pp. 251–421; J. Heyworth-Dunne, *An Introduction* ..., pp. 96–202; 'A. al-Rāfi'i, *'Aṣr Muḥammad 'Ali* (The Age of Muḥammad 'Ali), Cairo: 1947; pp. 356–363.
3. For a brief account of the traditional system of education, see J. Heyworth-Dunne, *An Introduction* ... , pp. 1–92.

In order for these first schools to be successful, certain basic problems had to be solved. The ensuing solutions set in motion a progression of changes, the momentum of which has not yet dissipated. Three problems were perhaps most important. First was the problem of obtaining qualified faculties. Egyptian education in the eighteenth century had been concerned chiefly with grammatical and theological studies. The educated persons engaged in teaching or available for such posts at the time of Muḥammad 'Ali had been trained in these fields and were relatively ignorant of the new subjects the latter wanted to introduce. Therefore, personnel to staff the new schools had to be drawn from outside sources. While occasionally a Turk or Syrian was able to meet the specifications, up to 1831 at least the chief source of personnel was European.[1]

The second problem Muḥammad 'Ali faced in his educational program was finding students who were willing to enter the schools, especially those in non-military fields. In addition to the apathy of early nineteenth-century Egyptians toward education there was a great deal of initial opposition to the recruitment of "native" Egyptians to the new schools of Muḥammad 'Ali. Inducements were therefore necessary to attract students during the early stages. By the 1830s, these attitudes seem to have undergone a profound transformation and there was often not enough space in the schools to accommodate all the would-be students.[2]

The third problem faced in the new schools was the provision of textbooks to supplement the lectures. Needless to say, original books written in Arabic on the new subjects were completely lacking. The only available texts were European books written in European

1. The quality of the European personnel was uneven, as would be expected. See the remarks on the poor quality of some of the European instructors, especially in the fields of medicine and related subjects, in P. N. Hamont, *L'Egypte sous Méhmét Ali*, Vol. II, Paris: 1843, pp. 108 ff.

2. A. 'Abd al-Karīm, *op. cit.*, pp. 31–34, summarizes the opposition of "native" Egyptians to the new schools. J. Bowring, in his *Report on Egypt and Candia Addressed to Lord Palmerstone*, London: 1840, pp. 125 ff., mentions the later overcrowding of the schools which indicated the change in the attitudes of Egyptians toward these educational institutions. See also M. A. Perron, "Lettre sur les écoles et l'imprimerie du Pasha d'Egypte," *Journal Asiatique*, Paris: 1843, pp. 5–23.

languages and designed for use in European institutions of higher learning. They were therefore incomprehensible to native students.

The early spectacle of the new schools must have bewildered the Egyptians who witnessed it. A European system of instruction in European subjects was transplanted to Egyptian soil, relying upon European teachers and texts. Nothing could have been more revolutionary. Had Muḥammad 'Ali chosen consciously to transform his society, he could scarcely have chosen a more effective path.

Muḥammad 'Ali's solutions to these three problems constituted a comprehensive program of education. To meet the problem of teaching personnel an alternative to European instructors had to be found. Muḥammad 'Ali felt that European instructors were a financial burden which Egypt could not afford indefinitely. In addition to their "huge" salaries, their employment required interpreters to translate their lectures. Thus they imposed a double salary requirement. Furthermore, the European instructors themselves complained of the ineffectiveness of the double-lecture system. One method of overcoming these difficulties was to substitute native teachers for European. The student missions to Europe sent by Muḥammad 'Ali were in part a means to this end.[1]

1. The first student mission was dispatched to Europe in 1809. It is known that between 1809 and 1826, a total of 28 students were sent to Italy, France, and England to study printing, naval construction, engineering, and related subjects. Of these 28 students we have detailed information about only two. The first was Niqūla Masābki who studied printing in Rome between 1815 and 1820 and acted as the first director of the Būlāq Press between 1821 and 1831. The second was 'Uthmān Nūr al-Dīn, who studied naval and military sciences in Italy and France between 1809 and 1817 and subsequently became "Admiral" of the Egyptian Navy. For information relating to these individuals and the early missions, see R. Cattaui. *Le règne de Mohamed Aly d'après les archives Russes en Egypte*, Cairo: 1931, Vol. I, pp. 387–388; Prisses d'Avennes and Hamont, *L'Egypte sous la domination de Méhmét Aly*, Paris: 1848, p. 142; A. al-Rāfi'i, *Ta'rīkh al-Ḥarakah al-Qawmīyah* (History of the Nationalist Movement), Vol. III, Cairo: 1930, pp. 452–453 and his *'Aṣr Muḥammad 'Ali*, pp. 346–348, 365–367; J. Heyworth-Dunne, *An Introduction* ... pp. 104–106.

More accurate information is available concerning the later student missions (1826–1863) in which about 408 students were sent abroad. Most of these students, 319, were sent between 1826 and 1848. Their subjects of specialization were as varied as Muḥammad 'Ali's ambitious schemes. Rough estimates can be given concerning the relative importance of these specialties (percentages are the author's computations):

Evidently Muḥammad 'Ali felt it would be more efficient in the long run to educate Egyptians abroad. He anticipated that, upon their return, they would gradually be able to replace the European instructors. In addition, they would have learned the foreign language faster and more thoroughly through their sojourn abroad.[1]

To meet the second problem – that of finding students – he launched a program of preparatory instruction divorced completely from the traditional *Kuttāb* system. Education was, needless to say, free. As a further inducement, monthly allowances were provided as well as clothing and, on the higher levels, lodging. The highest inducement, however, was the potential opportunity of joining the new Egyptian bureaucracy which was gradually emerging and which

---

Military and Naval Sciences	35%
Industrial Technique	27%
Engineering	18%
Medicine	7%
Administration, Law, Politics	6%
Agriculture and Agricultural Engineering	4%
Science (chemistry)	3%

The majority of those studying military and naval affairs were from the family of Muḥammad 'Ali.

For further details on these later student missions, their composition as well as their costs, see M. Jomard, "Ecole Egyptienne de Paris," *Journal Asiatique*, Paris: 1828, pp. 109–113; A. 'Abd al-Karīm, *op. cit.*, pp. 422–453; A. al-Rāfi'i, *'Aṣr Muḥammad*, pp. 367–380, and his *'Aṣr Ismā'īl* (The Age of Ismā'īl), Cairo: 1932, Vol. I, pp. 15, 45, and 215; and J. Heyworth-Dunne, *An Introduction* … , whose account of these missions is a most complete and comprehensive one, pp. 104–115, 221–223, 243–264, 288–301, 313–323. See also Amīn Sāmi, *Taqwīm al-Nīl* (The Nile Almanac), Vol. II, Cairo: 1928, pp. 595–621.

1. J. Heyworth-Dunne, *An Introduction* … , pp.157–158, states the problem in the following manner: "… the main reason for sending some forty students [the first large student mission] to France in order to acquire qualifications must be attributed to Muḥammad 'Ali's desire to dispense with the services of the Europeans who cost so much. To have had his own qualified subjects in charge of the various establishments would have been preferable, in his opinion, than the employment of Europeans who, with rare exception, had no particular tie in the country … The European official, as a rule, refused to learn Arabic or Turkish thus making it necessary for Muḥammad 'Ali either to supply large numbers of interpreters who were inefficient, or else to oblige the Turks and Egyptians to learn foreign languages." See further, J. Tājir, *op. cit.*, pp. 20–22.

offered respectable income and status.[1] A process of selection finally yielded enough students qualified for the new secular institutions of higher learning built by Muḥammad 'Ali.

Finally, to meet the problem created by the dearth of textbooks in Arabic, Muḥammad 'Ali began a number of projects which were to have a tremendous impact on both the translation movement itself and the broader movement of increased knowledge of the West. The first method utilized to deal with the textbook shortage was the translation into Arabic of numerous textbooks used in European – chiefly Italian and French – schools, and the reprinting of Turkish translations of similar works which had already appeared earlier in Constantinople.[2]

There is no evidence to suggest that there was an official centralized translation bureau where the bulk of the translating was being done. It has been stated, however, that a number of these translators were attached to the *Dīwān* of Muḥammad 'Ali and, similarly, that within the various departments of government there were individuals who translated books in addition to their regular administrative duties.[3]

A second device for obtaining textbooks in Arabic was the stipulation Muḥammad 'Ali attached to the student missions in Paris. The students were instructed to begin translating French textbooks into Arabic as soon as was feasible. These translations were to be sent immediately to Egypt for printing.

Initially, both devices led to unsatisfactory results, so far as Muḥammad 'Ali was concerned. The problems involved were too difficult to be surmounted by so haphazard an attack. First,

1. See M. Berger, *Bureaucracy and Society in Modern Egypt*, Princeton: 1957, pp. 21–22.

2. J. Zaydān, *Ta'rīkh ādāb al-Lughah al-'Arabīyah* (History of Arabic Literature), Vol. IV, Cairo: 1914, pp. 186–187, 190–191; and T. X. Bianchi, "Catalogue général des livres Arabes, Persans et Turcs imprimés à Boulac, en Egypte, depuis l'introduction de l'imprimerie dans ce pays," *Journal Asiatique*, Paris: 1843, pp. 24–61. Most of the works listed in this article are reprints of books that had been published earlier in Constantinople.

3. This was particularly true of the relatively well-known translators of this era, such as Ūghūst Sakākīni, 'Uthmān Nūr al-Dīn, Yūhanna 'Anḥūri, Yūsuf Far'ūn, and Yūsuf Būghuṣ. See Tājir, *op. cit.*, pp. 16–18.

competent translators were not available in sufficient numbers to take full advantage of the opportunities and inducements offered by Muḥammad 'Ali.[1] Furthermore, those individuals who were competent to undertake translations, regardless of quality, were overtaxed by the responsibilities given to them. They did not act as full-time translators but had to combine their translating activities with other administrative duties as well as with their official interpreting tasks. Perhaps because of their other preoccupations, their translations went slowly, too slowly it would appear to satisfy the demands of Muḥammad 'Ali. Two letters from Muḥammad 'Ali illustrate this point well. The first, addressed to a certain Jawāni in 1823, reads in part: "… concerning the medical books, we hereby order their translation from Italian into Arabic. It is further ordered that he should commence this work immediately and complete it with utmost dispatch. He should be warned that if he is negligent in his work he will be punished." In another letter, it was stated that: "… the books which … Saryūs translated arrived and were presented to the Benefactor [Muḥammad 'Ali]. When he showed these works to other translators they stated that the task could have been accomplished in eight and a half months … although the aforementioned translator received a salary approximating one hundred thousand piasters between 1827 up to the present [1832] … He had produced therefore six months [sic] worth of work in a five year period. For this reason an order was issued urging the aforementioned translator to exert himself more in the future."[2]

Muḥammad 'Ali was disappointed not only with the production of his local translators but also with the results of his first student missions. The demand that these students begin immediately to translate

1. It should be pointed out that knowledge of either Italian or French was limited to a handful of Egyptians. Both languages were introduced in elementary form into the new preparatory schools so that graduates would be able to pursue their medical studies abroad, but it was a long time before such graduates could begin to make their contribution. There was one "private" school, established by the Syrian, Umays al-Sama'āni, in 1829 which taught Arabic, French, and Italian. We possess no information concerning the persons who received education there or the importance of its influence on other educational developments. See J. Heyworth-Dunne, *An Introduction* … , pp. 271–272.

2. Both of these letters are quoted by Jāk Tājir, *op. cit.*, p. 22. See also R. R. Ṭahṭāwi, *Takhlīṣ al-Ibrīz ila Talkhīṣ Bārīz*, 3rd ed., Cairo: 1905, pp. 151–152.

textbooks was an unrealistic one to say the least. It reflected a lack of understanding on the part of Muḥammad 'Ali of both the difficulties of their studies and the prerequisites needed for translation. The students found that their studies precluded other activities such as translation. In addition, they lacked the background and even the knowledge of their field of study which would have been necessary for competent translating. Accordingly, what the students translated – and that in itself was very minimal – proved completely unsatisfactory to the ambitious Muḥammad 'Ali. This is borne out by the following letter sent to one of the students of the first mission. The letter stated: "He is to be reminded of the order given to him to send the geography books which he is translating ... volume by volume. He is reprimanded for stating that Mukhtār [another student] is still in the process of translating ... The necessity for giving in detail all information concerning what has already been translated ... attested by their supervisors is hereby emphasized. The students should hereafter give a detailed report at the end of each month on the quantity of translating which has been carried out during the month."

Having received a disappointing report about their progress, Muḥammad 'Ali scolded them in another letter in which he said: "... and are you not ashamed to excuse yourselves from translating the books which I ordered you to translate on the grounds of lack of time, which merely justifies your laziness." Partly to remedy this frustrating situation, he sent a letter to Clot Bey, then in Paris (1833), to the effect that he "should force the medical students to translate the books which they use as they go along and send the translations to Egypt."[1]

The students proved more useful after their return, however, than they had when still abroad. They seem to have been employed quite frequently as translators, simply translating their own textbooks. Because they were relatively numerous, they were not as overtaxed as their predecessors and were able or even obligated to devote full time to their labors. Most important, their competence in translation

1. All these quotations appear in the original Arabic in Tājir, *op. cit.*, pp. 25–26. See also Amīn Sāmi, *Taqwīm*, Vol. II, p. 414.

proved of superior quality. Almost all the important translators after 1831 – the date of the return of the first student mission – were products of the educational missions. They were, relative to their predecessors, better educated and possessed a greater command of the French language.[1]

During this relatively early period of random and somewhat haphazard translation activity, then, the major impetus for translation came from the desire to make available in Arabic western textbooks on a wide variety of subjects. During this period a cadre of personnel, trained abroad and, familiar with European languages, began to produce translations, most of which were technical in nature. The significance of this era lies chiefly in the foundation it laid for the third period in our division. It was during the third phase that the overwhelming bulk of the translations were executed under an organized and consistent program of governmental support.

Organized Period of Official Translation, 1835–1848

After the initial and relatively unfruitful phase of the translation effort which lasted through the year 1835, Muḥammad 'Ali decided to concentrate the translation work in a central organization under the direction of an official responsible for and empowered to control the entire project. This was accomplished with the inauguration of

1. One report of the treatment the returning students received mentions that all members of the first mission were locked up in the citadel in Cairo as soon as they returned and were given books to translate from French. They remained about three months in such "confinement." See Y. Artin, *L'Instruction publique en Egypte*, Paris: 1890, p. 73. Two episodes illustrate why the majority of the returning students were employed as translators: "The named Yūsuf … who had gone to Europe to study the manufacture of paper, returned after completing his studies, but he was unable to bring with him the necessary machinery and equipment. Until these can be brought he is to be entrusted with the translation of books … " As quoted by Tājir, *op. cit.*, p. 27. The other episode, related by Hamont and quoted by Heyworth-Dunne in *An Introduction* … , p. 168, is worth retelling. "One student on being asked what he had studied, replied 'Civil Administration.' 'And what is that?' asked Muḥammad 'Ali, to which the unfortunate student replied, 'the study of the government of affairs.' 'What!' exclaims Muḥammad 'Ali, 'you are not going to get mixed up in administration! what a waste of time! It is I who governs. Go to Cairo and translate military works.'" See Hamont, *op. cit.*, Vol. II, pp. 192–193.

the School of Translation in 1835 in Cairo. Two years later Rifā'ah al-Ṭahṭāwi was appointed director of the school. A "Bureau of Translation," also under the direction of Ṭahṭāwi, was set up within that school to serve as a central clearing house for all translated material.

With the centralization of translation activity, organization became possible and the entire movement reached its zenith, in terms of both personnel involved and output. Translators were numerous. Not only did students translate works as part of their language instruction but their teachers as well devoted themselves to translating. In addition, some of the professional translators were assigned to work under the auspices of the school.[1]

The quantity of works translated was prodigious, unmatched by any other period of translation during the nineteenth century in the Arab world. It has been reported that during this period more than two thousand works were translated into Arabic.[2] This figure may or may not be correct; it cannot be verified through the listings of official reference works. Yet, even though no exact count of the translations exists, there can be no doubt that their number was extremely large.

The quality of the translated works also improved due to the greater competence of the translators. Some indication of this is that during this period neither Muḥammad 'Ali nor members of his circle seem to have found fault with the translations although, as has been indicated above, criticism was quite common during the earlier period.

During this period of organized and controlled translation, the

1. For detailed information about the School of Languages, as it is commonly referred to, see Y. Artin, *op. cit.*, pp. 192 ff; A. Sāmi, *Taqwīm*, Vol. III, Part 1 (1936), pp. 13, 25, 34–35, 38; A. 'Abd al-Karīm, *op. cit.*, pp. 327–339; A. al-Rāfi'i, *'Aṣr Mūḥammad 'Ali*, pp. 394–395; J. Heyworth-Dunne, *An Introduction* … , pp. 150, 198, 220–221, 264–271; and Tājir, *op. cit.*, pp. 29–39. Most of these accounts give accurate and detailed information concerning the curriculum, personnel, students, and output of this school.

2. See the lists given in Shayyāl, *op. cit.*, p. 147 and Appendices I and II; see also Abū al-Futūḥ ⍰iḍwān, *Ta'rīkh Maṭba'at Būlāq* (History of the Bulaq Press), Cairo: 1953, pp. 446–479.

scope and range of the material rendered into Arabic widened; it was at this time that the eclectic variety of books described in the following chapter began to appear. This had both a short-term effect on later translations and a far-reaching effect on cultural developments in the entire Middle East.

This laudable effort, however, proved to be short-lived. It was almost entirely dependent upon the personality of Muḥammad 'Ali and upon the political fortunes of the Egyptian state. The military and political collapse of Muḥammad 'Ali devastated the educational system he had earlier launched. In fact, the virtual demise of that educational system might be counted as one of the severest casualties of the collapse of Muḥammad 'Ali's ambitious plans for Egypt. Because the translation movement formed such an integral part of the educational system, it, too, faced a grim future under the reign of the succeeding Viceroy, 'Abbās I.

The Decline of Official Translation, 1849–1863

The restrictive policies toward education of both 'Abbās I and Sa'īd, the Viceroy who succeeded him, were perhaps dictated by the necessity for conserving their financial resources.[1] In an age of ignorance, education undoubtedly lent itself more readily to such economizing than any other aspect of social significance. Since the *raison d'être* of the translation movement had been to furnish textbooks to the schools, the decline in the schools was accompanied by an even more serious decline in translation.

During the first two years of the reign of 'Abbās I, the School of Languages was not completely closed but was left to wither away from lack of support. It was officially closed in 1851 and with it, presumably, the Bureau of Translation. The translators who were part of the school were incorporated into other departments of the government.

1. The educational policies of 'Abbās I have aroused much controversy. Whether they were restrictive or not, the motives which lay behind the policies and the results of the policies have been debated and discussed in the literature. See the summary of the various points of view in Heyworth-Dunne, *An Introduction* ... , pp. 288–301, and see further al-Rāfi'i, *'Aṣr Ismā'īl*, Vol. I, pp. 3–22; Tājir, *op. cit.*, pp. 70–74; A. Sāmi, *Taqwīm*, Vol. III, Part I, pp. 13, 34–35, 438–439.

The school was not reopened until 1868 by order of Ismā'īl. During the intervening years little translation was done, but whatever was done was accomplished by the older graduates of the former School of Languages.[1]

The lack of book-length translations during these years does not indicate complete cessation of the translation movement, however. Due to the increased commercial transactions abroad, especially at the time of Sa'īd, there arose a need to translate legal documents relating to transactions of Europeans in Egypt. Partly to facilitate these European-Egyptian dealings, a Foreign Bureau was set up within the governmental structure. The services of translators were much in demand in both activities and, in a way, both were significant steps in the further development of the translation movement. The increased commercial and legal activities led ultimately to an increased interest in European works on legal and juridical subjects.[2] Had it not had this effect, this period would have to be classified as a total failure. The resuscitation of the translation movement, however, was left to the subsequent Khedive, Ismā'īl.

Revival of the Translation Movement and its Shift in Focus

Ismā'īl, perhaps as a result of his early upbringing in Europe among other reasons, was extremely interested in disseminating knowledge of the French language. To encourage wider knowledge of European languages he reopened the School of Languages in 1868, and the work of translation was organized and centrally directed anew.[3]

Under the benign auspices of Ismā'īl, then, the translation movement gained renewed vitality. Not only did the quantity of

1. J. Tājir quotes the order issued by 'Abbās I to close the school. He further-more gives some information on the subsequent fate of the translators. See his *op. cit.*, pp. 70–74. See also Shayyāl, *op. cit.*, pp. 142–144.

2. Zaydān, *Ta'rīkh* … , pp. 300–302.

3. As has been mentioned earlier, the school was reopened under the new name of School of Languages, Administration and Accountancy. It remained so named until 1886 when it became the School of Law, now part of Cairo University. See A. Sāmi, al-*Ta'līm* … , p. 20, pp. 91–92; A. al-Rāfi'i, *'Aṣr Ismā'īl*, Vol. I, p. 209; and Heyworth-Dunne, *An Introduction* … , pp. 267, 295–96, 327, 353, 389, and 392.

translations increase perceptibly but in addition they showed a new emphasis and direction. In place of the eclectic variety which had characterized the translations made during the era of Muhammad 'Ali, there was a concerted attempt to favor two specific fields. First, there was a noticeable increase in the number of purely military works which were translated into Arabic; second, there began the translating of complete European legal works.[1] It is interesting to note, for example, that the *Code Napoléon* and the French commercial code appeared at this time.[2]

The increased interest in legal works was undoubtedly related to the establishment of the Mixed Courts in Egypt (1876), where European languages – chiefly French – were official languages together with Arabic. It should be noted that this aspect of the translation movement had tremendous significance in view of later legal changes in the Arab world which derived much of their basis from these European legal documents. Further, these translations perhaps suggested to future Arab readers another aspect of European society worth studying. By the close of the nineteenth century, interest in the translation of French and English juridical writings was firmly established.[3]

The reign of Ismā'īl, which lasted until 1879, was the last period in the nineteenth century during which the translation of western books into Arabic and their publication were officially encouraged and supported by the Egyptian government. Afterwards, there was a noticeable decline in official concern with translation. Despite this

1. Zaydān, *op. cit.*, pp. 302–310; A. Al-Rāfi'i, *'Aṣr Ismā'īl*, Vol. I, pp. 293–294; J. Tājir, *op. cit.*, pp. 95–110. This latter work gives the titles of most of the works translated during this period. This list indicates the double preoccupation of Ismā'īl with military and legal treatises.

2. See below, p. 67, for the date of translation and publication of these works.

3. Most of the well-known translators of the latter part of the nineteenth century were associated with legal works. These were Ahmad Zaki, Fathi Zaghlūl, 'Abdullah Fikri, and others. Zaydān, *op. cit.*, pp. 306–310, gives short biographies of these men as well as an account of their legal contributions. Additional information is available in Tājir, *op. cit.*, pp. 125–134; and in al-Rāfi'i, *'Aṣr Ismā'īl*, Vol. I, pp. 293–295.

loss of public support, the translation movement continued unabated, its internal momentum generating new forces to carry out the work.

During the period of officially supported translation there gradually emerged a desire on the part of the educated groups within the Arab world to bring to the attention of the Arab reading public aspects of European art and literature. Without this, later translation might have perished. Furthermore, over the period there was a gradual shift from textbook translation toward more original works.[1] While initially the translated works had served primarily as texts for the schools of Muhammad 'Ali, this was not true of later translations. The latter, particularly in belles-lettres, jurisprudence, and social affairs, were gaining the upper hand in the field of translation by the end of the period we have been describing.

1. A comparison between the titles of works cited in the sources mentioned in footnote 1 above and those of works translated prior to 1870 (samples of which are presented in Chapter III of this study) reveals clearly the changing focus of the translations.

THREE

The Nature of the Translated Material

Muḥammad 'Ali's desire to establish a strong and viable Egyptian state led to his sending student missions abroad and establishing secular schools at home. The translation movement was inextricably connected with both these programs, recruiting its personnel primarily from the former and deriving its criterion of selection from the latter. Because of the close connection between the translation movement and the goals and policies of the state, the nature of the material translated from foreign languages constitutes a sensitive index to the type of awareness of western society which existed at various periods as well as to the relative values attached to specific western developments.

A word of caution must be introduced, however. Muḥammad 'Ali was interested in building a state, but it would be too much to presume that he knew the best means for doing so. He was dependent upon both his advisers and the executors of his policies for the development of means. He gave the orders, but it was they who had to implement them to the best of their abilities and intellectual capacities. In the process of implementation, changes occurred and new directions were pursued which neither he nor others could have predicted in advance. Therefore, the real content of his program was the product of the agents of his directives. Among these was al-Shaykh Rifā'ah Rāfi' al-Ṭahṭāwi, the moving spirit of the entire translation movement and, consequently, one of the most important figures in the nineteenth century's growing Arab awareness of the West.[1]

1. We have emphasized here, perhaps too strongly, the role of Ṭahṭāwi. This emphasis is based on the nature of our conception of the interaction of the western and Arab worlds during the period in question. Our concern is with the "humanist" rather than the "technical" nature of the interaction, since this humanist aspect has

A more balanced perspective on early nineteenth-century westernization in the Arab world can be gained if we look not only at Muḥammad 'Ali but also at R. Ṭahṭāwi. The first witnessed the manifestations of another society and deliberately tried to emulate it; the second perceived, relatively speaking, the complexity of the process and the breadth and depth of the other culture. The first concentrated on the techniques to be adopted; the second had greater insight into the relationship between specific techniques and the rest of the social organization. The effects of Ṭahṭāwi's sophistication are revealed when the translations themselves are analyzed.

Translations Undertaken

The pragmatic, technical interests of Muḥammad 'Ali have been stressed so frequently that one often loses sight of the fact that not all the western works translated into Arabic under his auspices were military or scientific manuals. While it is true that such works predominated and that, with few exceptions, technical works appeared in translation earlier than studies in other fields,[1] it is also true that a wide variety of books in history and the arts were rendered into Arabic during his reign.

Nor is there any evidence that Muḥammad 'Ali begrudged the translation of such non-military and non-technical books, even though he himself may have been baffled by them. The rewards bestowed on translators of these kinds of works were no less than

been previously neglected in the literature on the nineteenth century. There is no doubt that in that particular area Tahtāwi was the outstanding figure of his day. Furthermore, he was one of the few "native" Egyptians to distinguish himself during the early period of Muḥammad 'Ali's reign. The rewards – in terms of financial payment and appointments to responsible positions – which were bestowed upon him by Muḥammad 'Ali reflect the high degree of appreciation the latter felt for his work. On this point, see A. al-Rāf'i, *'Aṣr Muḥammad 'Ali*, Cairo: 1947, pp. 383–395 and compare with pp. 395–399; A. A. Badawi, *Rifā'ah al-Ṭahṭāwi*, Cairo: 1950, pp. 34–35; J. Heyworth-Dunne, "Rifā'ah Badawi Rafi' at-Ṭahṭāwi, The Egyptian Revivalist," *BSOS*, London: 1939, Vol. IX, pp. 961–967; and Vol. x, pp. 400 ff.

1. Compare, for example, the list of works given by Zaydān in his *Ta'rīkh*, Vol. IV, pp. 188–191 with the list prepared for this chapter. The works of the earliest translators, Muharram Bey, 'Uthmān Nūr al-Dīn and Ibrāhīm Adham, all dealing with technical subjects, appeared in the 1830s or very early 1840s.

those granted to the translators of technical manuals.[1] And, in addition, there is some evidence to suggest that Muḥammad 'Ali himself selected for translation certain books which had no tangible connection with the technical aspects of the West.[2] His support of the School of Languages and of the students who later graduated from it is ample proof of his desire for translations of all kinds.

At the head of this School of Languages, which was to play a vital role in the transmission of western ideas, Muḥammad 'Ali placed the most competent of his early translators, Ṭahṭāwi, whose task was nothing less than to supervise all work being done in the field of translation. After 1837, Ṭahṭāwi even seems to have been given the power to select the material to be translated. His power was circumscribed in reality by both the explicit and implicit wishes of the Viceroy. To placate Muḥammad 'Ali or perhaps to consolidate his position with the Viceroy, Ṭahṭāwi continued the previous policy of selection by favoring technical works. However, it was at this time that non-technical books began to receive more attention by the translators.

Since practically all works translated during the ensuing period were explicitly intended for use as textbooks in the schools of

1. All biographies of the translators bear out this fact. See J. Tājir, *Ḥarakat al-Tarjamah bi Miṣr*, Cairo: 1945, for a brief account; also al-Rāfi'i, *'Aṣr Ismā'īl*, Vol. I, pp. 219, 268, 270, 272 and 279 *seq*. It is reported that when a translator had completed his work, whether or not he had previously been ordered to render it into Arabic, he presented it to Muhammed 'Ali in expectation of a reward. As an illustration, see the introduction to Ḥ. Qāsim, *Ta' rīkh Mulūk Faransa*, Cairo: 1847, pp. 2–3.

2. Enfantin, in a letter to his friend Arles dated January 13, 1836, claimed that Muḥammad 'Ali had ordered the translation of E. Barrault's book, *Occident et Orient*, published in Paris in 1836, after it had been brought to his attention. As a result of this order one of the translators approached Enfantin to obtain a copy of the original French version because it was unavailable in Muḥammad 'Ali's library. See *Oeuvres d'Enfantin*, Paris: 1872, p. 236.

Another letter, sent by Muḥammad 'Ali in 1827 to one of his early "representatives" in London, clearly conveyed his eclectic interest in western material. He wrote, "It has been brought to Our attention that an English book has been published showing the costs of every government ship built by the British State. Also, there are printed books composed in a simple manner from which children learn eagerly. Accordingly, Our will is hereby given, directing you to purchase the aforementioned works … and bring them [to Egypt]." Quoted in J. Tājir, *op. cit.*, p. 17 (translation ours). See also H. Abū al-Su'ūd, *Nazm al-La'āli' fi al-Sulūk fi man Ḥakam Faransa min al- Mulūk*, Cairo: 1841, pp. 3–4.

Muḥammad ʿAli, the activities of the Bureau of Translation were divided to correspond to the divisions in the educational system. The four major sections of the Bureau were the division of mathematical translation, the division of medical and physical (physics) translation, the division of literary (*adabīyāt*) translation, and the division of Turkish translation, in which military manuals were translated into Turkish for use by Ottoman soldiers in the Egyptian army. One significant aspect of this division is that non-technical works evidently received official sanction and, indeed, there was a separate division of the Bureau devoted exclusively to their translation.[1]

It was within the literary division that most of the translations of European (primarily French) non-technical works were accomplished. Samples are given below of the types of works translated in the division of literary translations. Among the subjects covered were: history and biography; philosophy and logic; geography and travel; politics; "anthropology"; and literature or belles-lettres. The following list is arranged in chronological order within each subject heading.

List of Translations

HISTORY AND BIOGRAPHY

1833 *Taʾrīkh Dawlat Iṭālya* (A History of Italy), by M. Botta. Translated by ʿAbdullah ʿAzīz and Ḥasan Effendi.

1836 *Bidāyat al-Qudamāʾ wa Hidāyat al-Ḥukamāʾ* (The Origins of the Ancients and the Guidance of the Sages), an ancient history of Greece, Rome, and the Near East. This was not a direct translation of any one volume but rather an "assimilation" of several works. Translated by Muṣṭafa al-Zarābi *et al.*

1840 *Qurrat al-Nufūs wa al-'Uyūn Bisiyar Ma Tawassaṭ min al-Qurūn* (Comforts of the Souls and Eyes in Events in Medieval Times). This history of the Middle Ages appeared in two volumes and, like the preceding reference,

1. A. ʿAbd al-Karīm, *op. cit.*, pp. 341–342. On the basis of original material available in the Egyptian Archives, the author discusses the problems that led ultimately to this division.

was not a literal translation of a single book. Translated by Muṣṭafa al-Zarābi.

1841 *Naẓm al-La'āli' fi al-Sulūk fi man Ḥakam Faransa min al-Mulūk* (The Arrangement of Gems Concerning French Monarchs). Translated by Ḥasan Abū al-Su'ūd.[1]

1841 *Maṭali' Shumūs al-Siyar fi Waqā'i' Kārlūs al-Thāni 'Ashar (Histoire de Charles XII, Roi de Suède)* written originally by François Voltaire. Translated by M. M. Bayyā'.

1841 *Ithāf al-Mulūk al-Alibbā' bi Taqaddum al-Jam'īyāt bi Bilād Ūrubba,* a direct translation of Volume I of *The History of the Reign of the Emperor Charles the Fifth,* written by William Robertson. The Arabic translation by 'Abduh Khalīfah Maḥmūd was made from the French version. The entire study of four volumes was translated but the three remaining volumes were not published until nine years later (see below).

1842 *Burhān al-Bayān wa Bayān al-Burhān fi Istikmāl wa Ikhtilāl Dawlat al-Rūmān.* This was a direct translation of *Considérations sur les causes de la grandeur des Romains et de leur décadence,* written by Montesquieu and published in France in 1734. It was translated into Arabic by Ḥ. al-Jubayli.

1847 *Ta'rīkh Mulūk Faransa* (History of the French Monarchs). Translated by Ḥasan Qāsim. The French author of the original study cannot be determined. The Arab translator transliterated his name as Mūniqūrūs.[2]

---

1. The original French version cannot be determined. See the following footnote for further information.

2. This work and the volume translated earlier by Ḥ. Abū al-Su'ūd (1841) were significant from two points of view. First, they were among the first translated works to deal with the history of a European nation. And second, and most important from the standpoint of our study, they were the chief sources of information concerning the French Revolution in the pre-1870 Arab world. In terms of accuracy and detail, they were to remain, up to 1870, the principal sources of information on the history, development and principles of the French Revolution. See Ḥ. Abū al-Su'ūd, *Naẓm*, pp. 180–205, and Qāsim, *Ta'rīkh* … , pp. 242–341.

It should be noted that in both these accounts, the term used to describe the form of government which emerged after the abolition of the French monarchy was

1849 *al-Rawḍ al-Azhar fi Ta'rīkh Buṭrus al-Akbar* (Histoire de l'empire de Russie sous Pierre le Grand), written by François Voltaire. Translated by Aḥmad 'Ubayd al-Ṭahṭāwi.

1850 *Itḥāf Mulūk al-Zamān bi Ta'rīkh al-Imbarāṭur Shārlikān.* These were the final three volumes of the translation of Robertson's study of the history of Charles V, cited above.[1]

PHILOSOPHY AND LOGIC

1836 *Ta'rīkh al-Falāsifah* (History of the Philosophers); no original source or author is given. Translated by 'Abdullah Ḥusayn.

1843 *al-Mushriq bi 'ilm al-Manṭiq,* a literal translation of *Logique* by C. de Dumarsais rendered by A. Khalīfah Maḥmūd.

GEOGRAPHY AND TRAVEL

1843 *al-Jughrāfiyah al-'Umūmīyah*, a literal translation of C. Malte-Brun's original work, *Précis de la Géographie Universelle*, published in six volumes in France between 1810 and 1829. Three of these volumes were translated by R. R. Ṭahṭāwi.

1843 *al-Ta'rībāt al-Shāfiyah li-Murīd al-Jughrāfiyah* (The Complete Translation for the Seeker of Geography). This was evidently not a direct translation but rather an "assimilation" of several books by R. R. Ṭahṭāwi.[2]

1845 *Siyāḥah fi Amrīka*, a literal translation of *Travels in America* by H. Markham translated by Sa'd Ni'ām.

1848 *Siyāḥah fi al-Hind*, a literal translation of *Travels in India* by H. Thorolde, translated by Ibrāhīm al-Bayyā'.

1869 *al-Dars al-Mukhtaṣar al-Mufid fi'ilm al-Jughrāfiyah al-Jadīd* (A Brief and Useful Lesson in the New Geography).

Jumhūrīyah, i.e., Republic. The reader is referred to Chapter 1 of this study for further elaboration on the terminological question.

1. This work, particularly the explanatory remarks of the translator which appear in it, is especially significant and will be treated in more detail in Chapter VII.

2. This is another significant volume which receives some attention in Chapter VII.

No original source identification is given by the translator, Ḥ. Abū al-Su'ūd.

POLITICS

1832 *Kitāb al-Amīr* (The Book of the Prince). This was a translation by an Italian, Don Raphael, of Machiavelli's *The Prince*. No copies of this work are extant, which leads us to believe either that it was printed in a limited edition or that it never reached the stage of publication. A copy of the original manuscript is preserved in the Egyptian Archives.

ANTHROPOLOGY

1833 *Qalā'id al-Mafākhir fi' Awā'id al-Awā'il wa al-Awākhir*, a direct translation of *Aperçu historique sur les moeurs et coutumes des nations* by G. Depping, rendered into Arabic by R. R. Ṭahṭāwi.

LITERATURE

1850 *Mawāqi' al-Aflāk fi Waqā'i' Talīmāk*, a direct translation of *Les aventures de Télémaque* by Fénelon published originally in France in 1717. This work was translated by R. R. Ṭahṭāwi in two editions, the last in 1867.

1850 *Riwāyat al-Shāykh Matlūf,* a translation of the Molière play, *Tartuffe,* prepared by 'Uthmān Jalāl.

1850 *al-'Uyūn al-Yawāqiz fi al-Amthāl wa al-Mawā'iz,* a translation of La Fontaine's *Fables* by 'Uthmān Jalāl.[1]

---

1. This translator is credited with being the "father" of the short story in Arabic. The two translations by Jalāl cited here are by no means his only contributions. He translated a number of works by famous French authors such as Molière, Racine, and La Fontaine. See I. Sarkīs, *Mu'jam al-Maṭbū'āt al-'Arabīyah wa al-Mu'arrabah* (Dictionary of Arabic Bibliography), Cairo: 1928, p. 1306. See also L. Shaykhu, *al-Ādāb al-'Arabīyah fi al-Qarn al-Tāsi' 'Ashar* (Arabic Literature in the Nineteenth Century), Vol. II, Beirut: 1924, pp. 2, 100–102; J. Zaydān, *Ta'rīkh*, p. 245; M. 'Abd al-Rāziq, "Arabic Literature since the Beginning of the Nineteenth Century," in *BSOS*, London: 1921, Vol. II, pp. 256–257; and C. Brockelmann, *Geschichte der Arabischen Litteratur*, Leyden: 1938, Vol. II, pp. 476–477.

It should be noted, however, that his works were not the first translations of

LAW

1867 *Qānūn Yata'allaq bi Niẓām wa Tartīb al-Mashyakhah al-Baladīyah fī Bārīs,* a translation in three volumes of the Napoleonic Code.[1]

The Content of the Translations

The above is only a partial listing of the literary works which were translated from European languages into Arabic during the first seven decades of the nineteenth century.[2] A comprehensive list would be neither possible nor essentially useful. We were limited by the need to examine the concrete information transmitted through this channel of cultural exchange. Many of the other works are unavailable, and since not even the total number of non-technical translations is known, we cannot estimate the extent to which our list begins to approach completeness. Yet even this limited sample offers us the opportunity to establish some of the concrete information a literate Arab of the nineteenth century could have derived about the West from books written by westerners and translated into his own tongue.

Such a reader (especially one trained in the new schools of Muḥammad 'Ali, but not necessarily confined to this group) would

European plays and novels. He was preceded in this endeavor by the Lebanese Mārūn al-Naqqāsh (1817–1855). For further information on this man, see I. Sarkīs, *op. cit.*, p. 1867; Zaydān, *Tarājim Mashāhīr al-Sharq fī al-Qarn al-Tāsi' 'Ashar* (Eastern Celebrities in the Nineteenth Century), Cairo: 1922, third edition, Vol. II, pp. 231 ff.; and A. Dāghir, *Maṣādir al-Dirāsah al-Adabīyah*, (Sources of Literary Studies), Beirut: 1955, Vol. II, pp. 748–751.

1. See below, p. 145.

2. For a list of selected technical works given in a similar compact form, see E. C. Van Dyke, *Iktifā' al-Qanū' fī Māhuwa Matbū'* (The Sufficient Guide to the Contented on What Is Printed), Cairo: 1897, pp. 422–438, 454–462; Zaydān, *Ta'rīkh*, pp. 192–199, 209–217; and M. 'Abd al-Rāziq's article in the *BSOS* cited above, pp. 253–254. It should be noted that historians of the translation movement did not deal with it topically but only chronologically, for example, J. Tājir, *op. cit.* The quasi-systematic treatment of Zaydān, *Ta'rīkh*, pp. 186–311, is topical (viz. Medical, Physical, Mathematical) but little attention is paid to the chronology. In the sample list presented in this chapter, on the other hand, an attempt was made to isolate the "humanist" literature by topic and date of publication to show its intimate connection with the remainder of the translation movement.

have gained a historical background about the evolution of western society. The main characteristics of important historical epochs, of important literary and military figures, and the major outlines of European political development were fast becoming a part of the background knowledge of the educated segment of Arab society.

Such a reader would also have had available to him a concrete image of the political, economic and natural geography of the world. The location and characteristics of European countries and, indeed, the remainder of the world in so far as it was known to European scholars, were made a part of his own *weltanschauung*. He was no longer dependent on the inaccuracies of the traditional geographical works written by medieval Arab geographers.

Such a reader would have been able to gain an impression, albeit a rather superficial one, of Greek philosophy and philosophers, explained in relatively uncomplicated language. Thus he would have been able to gain a certain familiarity with names and basic concepts. The previous suppression of philosophical works during the Arab "Dark Ages" had precluded that familiarity. Similarly, the basic principles of logic were made available to the Arab reader during the early nineteenth century.

Perhaps most significantly, an Arab reader would have been able to expand and deepen his knowledge about the West. On the social side, he had available to him information concerning western customs, manners, and traditions. On the artistic side, the books implanted an awareness of and a taste for French literature which had far-reaching effects on the evolution of Arabic literature. And finally, on the political side, the Arab reader delving into the translated works would have developed an awareness of the distinct European nations in both a geographic and historical sense. The previous assumption that all Europeans could be classified simply as "Christians" or "Franks" was no longer tenable for educated Arabs.[1]

1. The observation of H. A. R. Gibb is pertinent. He stated: "In Egypt the principal sources from which European thought was radiated were the technical schools founded by Muḥammad 'Ali, and the educational missions which he dispatched to Europe. These schools, modelled on European lines, often under European supervision, had as their first aim the training of doctors, administrators,

The image which could be derived from a complete study of these translated works was still extremely fragmentary and imperfect. It could not have been otherwise, considering the paucity of existing information prior to the translations. There was a preponderance of historical and geographical translations. This can be explained in part by the value placed upon such knowledge, but also in part by the fact that these kinds of works presented fewer difficulties both for the translator and for his audience. The problem of adapting foreign terminology and concepts was not as severe here as it was in certain other fields of the arts, notably philosophy and literature. Despite the fact that Arab awareness of the West was therefore more pronounced in historical and geographical aspects than in others, it should not be forgotten that these studies in themselves gave a glimpse of western political systems and principles, a fact which had important consequences for subsequent developments in the Arab world.

Conspicuously absent from the lists of translations made prior to 1870 are works dealing with pure science, philosophy (the subject itself rather than a history of ancient philosophy), political theory, and jurisprudence, to mention but a few. However, after 1870 there occurred a major shift in the subject matter of translation.

While up to 1870 the center of translation had been Egypt and the chief figures involved in the translation movement Egyptian, after that date the important translators were Syrians (i.e. from the Fertile Crescent) functioning either in Syria itself or in Egypt. A shift in the nature of the translated material went hand in hand with this shift in personnel. During the period following 1870 the substance of the translation movement had become preponderantly

---

lawyers and technical experts of all kinds who were necessary for the carrying out of the Pasha's ambitious projects. It was inevitable that many of the graduates should be attracted towards other sides of western culture than those which they were primarily studying, more especially towards French literature." See Gibb, "Studies in Contemporary Arabic Literature," in *BSOS*, London: 1928, Vol. IV, p. 748. Whether or not the students of technical subjects developed such an interest in literature cannot be substantiated. Clearly they left no evidence of so wide a view. Translations of literary works were made only by the students of the School of Languages. It is their output which must be considered the principal source for the transmission of European thought and culture, a fact which Gibb acknowledges later in the same article.

belleletttristic, and it was to continue in that vein on into the twentieth century.[1]

There was also another important shift in the focus of the translated works. By the latter part of the nineteenth century a number of works began to appear dealing with western jurisprudence, sociology, and politics. Although the quantity of these works was not large, their quality was vastly superior to the earlier translations. In these fields, the major translators were Egyptian.[2]

Other Translators of the Nineteenth Century

Thus far we have concentrated on the work performed by the professional Egyptian translators who monopolized the field for the greater part of the period. The shortcomings of the material they translated – both unbalanced selection and poor quality – can be attributed to the inadequacies of the translators themselves. The subject matter was so new that the translators often lacked the background necessary to obtain a real understanding of their subject. In addition, the translators were relatively unfamiliar with the wide gamut of literature available in the foreign tongues and could therefore not always make the most judicious choice among available sources.

Unhindered by these handicaps was another group of translators who ideally could have brought to the task a greater and more sophisticated understanding of the West than could any Arab. These were the foreign missionaries operating in Lebanon for the most part. These missionaries were westerners often deeply dedicated to the education of their flocks. One would anticipate that they might have

1. For an illustration of this, see A. Dāghir, *op. cit.*, pp. 789–839. The works of Salīm al-Bustāni (1848–1884), Sulaymān al-Bustāni (1856–1925) who was the translator of Homer's *Iliad*, of Najīb al-Ḥaddād (1867–1899), and of Faraḥ Anṭūn (1874–1922), not to mention the literary output of Zaydān, illustrate this point clearly. Most of these post-1870 personalities were Syrian but they worked in Egypt as well as Syria. See also Zaydān, *Ta'rīkh* pp. 189–193, 300–304.

2. The works of the Egyptians Ahmad Zaki, Fatḥi Zaghlūl (translator of Bentham's *Principles of Legislation*, and works by Gustave Le Bon and others), and their colleagues all appeared at the turn of the century. See J. Zaydān, *Ta'rīkh*, pp. 304–318; and Dāghir, *op. cit.*, pp. 422–427, 412–416.

been able to translate or transmit a balanced and well-rounded image of the West.

This did not prove to be the case. Close scrutiny of their contribution indicates that they fell into the same pattern as did Muḥammad ʿAli. They were chiefly preoccupied with translating or writing textbooks to be used in their schools. Practically all of their works were of a technical nature – if we exclude theological tracts – dealing with elementary mathematics, chemistry, and geography.[1] It is almost impossible to trace any other type of work which they translated into Arabic.

Thus, if we conclude that the indigenous translators were interested chiefly in learning about the techniques and "know-how" of the West, we must equally conclude that westerners were chiefly interested in conveying this aspect of western culture to the Arab East. In our view, neither conclusion is completely warranted. What happened during this early period of rediscovery of the West was that an attempt was made first to fill the most glaring gaps in the indigenous culture in an attempt to spark its evolution. Since the "technical" aspects of life were most conspicuously absent, they received priority. Later, after some of this urgency had been dissipated, other areas, namely the nature of the society which had produced such techniques, could be explored at greater leisure.

A Digression on Ninth- and Nineteenth-Century Translation

It is well known that the Arabs eagerly adapted the works of the ancient Greeks during the ninth century. That story of cultural transmission hardly needs retelling. The similarities and the differences in the kinds of works translated by Arabs during that earlier period and during the nineteenth century are illuminating and reveal the levels of cultural awareness and the degree of curiosity exhibited by the Arabs of both periods.

The striking fact about the translations of the ninth century was that they covered a wide area of knowledge, with three notable

1. See the list of works translated by American missionaries given in E. C. Van Dyke, *op. cit.*, pp. 401–403, and 453, for confirmation of this point.

exceptions – literature, theology, and history. On the other hand, Greek science, philosophy, logic, mathematics, zoology, botany, astronomy, and related fields all became part of the legacy of medieval Arabs.[1]

By comparison, nineteenth-century interest in translation was more limited. Technical works were its chief concern, and these technical works were rarely "pure science." Geography and history were secondary emphases, while minor attention was paid to literature and law. Philosophy, logic, and science in its pure sense received virtually no attention.

The neglect of these latter areas during the nineteenth century has never been adequately explored in terms of its relation to the subsequent evolution of Arab intellectual endeavours. Most students of western culture agree that it was the revolution in the basic sciences and, with it, the revolution in the philosophy of knowledge that underlay the social institutions which developed in the modern West. But as we have noted, these were the very areas of western culture which were not transmitted to the Arab world through translation. In a way, the superstructure of the cultural manifestations was transmitted but not the intellectual bent of mind which in the West had led to its establishment. We can speculate, therefore, that the early nineteenth-century transmission of European knowledge had only a limited immediate effect on the intellectual outlook of the Arab world. It introduced superficial changes but did not shake the foundations of Arab society as that Arab society had been shaken during the ninth century.

Justifications for the Translations

The motivations behind the translation of technical works directed by Muḥammad 'Ali were relatively simple. The books were needed for training technically proficient persons to perform in the army, navy, industry, and agriculture. The same was the case for the translation of material dealing with medicine and "science." Indigenous literature in these fields could offer no substitute for the foreign sources.

1. See P. K. Hitti, *History of the Arabs*, New York: 1951 (5th ed.), pp. 309–316.

The motivation for translating non-technical works, however, was somewhat more complex and obscure. Why were certain non-technical books selected for translation? It is begging the question to reply that they were deemed necessary as texts in the schools of Muḥammad 'Ali.[1] Why were they considered necessary? Why was it deemed desirable for Arab students to study European history and geography, and why were these subjects included in the curriculum of the schools?

No explicit answer to these questions can be found either in the writings of the time or in the explanatory notes of the translators. We might hypothesize that the utilitarian motive was less strong than it was in the purely technical works. Rather, the real object of such studies, and therefore of the translated works, seems to have been to obtain a better understanding of the West which had inspired awe and respect in Muḥammad 'Ali and the men surrounding him. This hypothesis would be purely conjectural if it were not for the proven influence of Ṭahṭāwi, whose genuine interest in the West and western learning is verified in his works and deeds.[2]

A meager source of our knowledge about the translators' motivations is the information the translators themselves sometimes provided. Usually their justifications were general: they translated particular works because they were widely used in French schools or because they were "beneficial". Sometimes, however, the translators were more specific. A few illustrations may suggest their frame of mind.

In the introduction to an ancient history, for example, the translators state that "history is the counsel of every Prince, and the prince of every counsel … from which virtuous souls derive rest and from which perfect souls – be they sages or masters, kings or sultans – may learn." They note that the book contains information desired by Muḥammad 'Ali, "whose abiding interest in history is great and whose curiosity about earlier monarchs is equally strong … The history of those periods, especially Greek history, is extremely deficient

1. See Ṭahṭāwi's introduction to *al-Ta'rībāt al-Shāfiyah li-Murīd al-Jughrāfiyah*, pp. 2–4, in which he stated that the volume was to be used specifically in the schools as a basic textbook in geography.

2. This is substantiated later in Chapters V and VI.

in Arabic." Therefore, both the interest in history and the existing deficiency of the literature are cited as motives for its selection.[1]

A translated book on medieval European history was intended to complete the picture of history begun in the above-mentioned work. In the introduction to that work, the translator noted that: "This is a treatise in the history of the Middle Ages, a continuation of the ancient history which our Benefactor has already allowed to be published … It is a valuable work in its intent, useful to those interested and from which one can learn about the conditions of medieval times."[2]

Still another translator justified his efforts in the following manner: "I had a great desire to translate this work, especially because it combined two important aims: first, the history of Charles V, and second, the unveiling of the great events and the tremendous revolutions which took place in a great area of the globe, namely Europe, which moved from the most extreme degree of barbarism to the highest peak of civilization and happiness … It is also important for anyone wanting to learn about the administration of vast realms [the reference here is undoubtedly to Muḥammad 'Ali] and about political principles …"[3]

A translator of a work by Voltaire recounted that his particular book was selected for translation by R. Ṭahṭāwi both because of its subject matter and the importance of its author. "It is the history of a Frankish king whose fame rises higher than Mars. It is the history of Peter the Great whose virtue in the European realms is too well-known to be mentioned … [The book is especially important] since its author is one of the greatest of French philosophers … namely Voltaire … who is considered by philosophers to be the greatest authority."[4]

As a final example we might cite the following: "This is a competent translation of a most difficult French historical work to which the rest of the European nations pay close attention. Nay, each nation

1. M. al-Zarābi, *Bidāyat al-Qudamā' wa Hidāyat al-Ḥukamā'*, pp. 3–5.
2. M. Zarābi, *Qurrat al-Nufūs wa al-'Uyūn Bisiyar Ma Tawassat min al-Qurūn*, p. 2.
3. 'A. K. Maḥmūd, *Itḥāf al-Alibbā' bi Taqaddum al-Jam'īyāt bi Bilād Ūrubba*, Vol. I, pp. 6, 9.
4. Aḥmad 'A. Ṭahṭāwi, *al-Rawḍ al-Azhar fi Ta'rīkh Buṭrus al-Akbar*, pp.2–3.

which is inclined toward struggle (*Jihād*) must consider it very carefully … for from it one derives much benefit because of the strange events which transpired whereby one of the great European monarchs acquired glorious honor in the field of battle … especially the honors which he [Charles XII of Sweden] … derived from his struggle against the Muscovite Czar, Peter the Great."[1]

These themes appear in various forms in almost all the translated works of this nature. On the basis of their introductory remarks it is difficult to isolate exactly what the translators or their sponsor had in mind. All that can be stated with accuracy is that there was a certain amount of interest and curiosity about European history. A decided preoccupation with European leaders who attained military and political power can definitely be identified, a preoccupation which must be traced to Muḥammad 'Ali's fascination with the exploits of great historical models of effectiveness.

The Impact of the Translations on Arab Intellectual Development

There can be little doubt that the translated works had an important effect on the subsequent literary history of the Arabs.[2]

The impact is difficult to assess concretely, however. We will indicate here only the most tangible elements of this impact, which are apparent in three major categories – content, method, and style.

We have already alluded to the content of the works which were translated into Arabic. Western ideas were undoubtedly planted; but their impact depended on the degree to which they were comprehended and assimilated. Similarly, concrete knowledge of geography and of the major physical resources of the West was

1. M. M. Bayyā', *Maṭāli' Shumūs al-Siyar fi Waqā'i' Kārlūs al-Thāni 'Ashar*, pp. 3–4.
2. See the informative articles of H. A. R. Gibb: "Studies in Contemporary Arabic Literature," *BSOS*, Vol. IV, pp. 745–761; Vol. V, pp. 311–322 and pp. 445–466; Vol. VII, pp. 1–22. See also I. Kračkovskij, "Der Historische Roman in der Neuren Arabischen Literatur," in *Die Welt des Islam*, Band 12, Berlin: 1930, pp. 52–87; H. Pérès, "Les premières manifestations de la renaissance littéraire Arabe en Orient au XIXe siècle," *Annales de l'Institut d'Etudes Orientales*, Faculté des Letteres de l'Université d'Alger, Vol. I, 1934–35, pp. 233–256 and his "Le roman, Le conte et La nouvelle dans la littérature Arabe moderne," in *Annales*, Vol. III, 1937, pp. 266–333.

transmitted. To this must be added the knowledge which was the product of the technical translations. Thus, in terms of content, a fairly complete if unbalanced image of the western world was available upon which understanding and assessment of the West could be grounded.

A by-product of the translation movement was the respect for western scholarship it generated among Arab men of letters, respect which was generalized to many other fields of learning. As a result of this, the works of western orientalists began to be translated into Arabic. The first such work to be translated was *Nihāyat al-Arab fi Ta'rīkh al-'Arab,* based on a work by the French orientalist Sédillot, which appeared in Arabic in 1872.[1] Other works were to follow. Thus Arabs not only viewed the West through western eyes but also began to view themselves through those same eyes.

The impact of the translations on Arab methodology is even clearer. A brief comparison between late nineteenth- and early twentieth-century literature and that of the preceding period clearly reveals some basic changes. The earlier works appear to the western reader to be capriciously ordered collections of heterogeneous thoughts. In contrast, the later works are comparatively well organized in their presentation. It is also important to note that, in the writings of the latter half of the nineteenth century, a concerted attempt was made by authors to concentrate on the content and meaning of their books and to be less exclusively preoccupied with the decorative aspects of verbal play. The latter had been one of the chief characteristics of Arabic writing prior to that time. Perhaps another effect was a somewhat more critical approach to learning as such, but even at this writing that change is still in embryonic form.

We have alluded above to the stylistic changes apparent in contemporary Arabic literature. These can be traced in part at least to the translation of western books which, by their nature, did not lend themselves readily to poetic flights of fancy. Beginning with the nineteenth century, the *Saj'* (rhyming) form of prose began

1. This book was translated by M. A. 'Abd al-Rāziq. The original work appeared under the title, *Histoire des Arabes*, Paris: 1854.

to be discarded because it was not in the original European works. Subsequent original writers may have found the new form easier to imitate, but irrespective of the exact reason it became more acceptable. By the twentieth century it had become the usual style of composition.

Other stylistic changes may also be identified. For example, punctuation marks became firmly entrenched in Arabic composition during the last century, an important departure from earlier works. Intelligible titles also began to replace earlier title forms in which wit and rhyme substituted for sense. Today it is almost impossible to find works in Arabic where the title does not convey, in at least rough form, the content of the volume.[1]

The modern revival of Arabic literature, the purification and simplification which made it a new medium of thought and communication, cannot be entirely explained without reference to the impact of the nineteenth-century translation movement. The nature of that literature was enriched by the addition of a new form of literary prose as well as by new approaches to law, politics, history, and geography, not to mention technical subjects, which can be directly ascribed to the early translation movement. This movement which Muḥammad 'Ali initiated outlived him, but to him and to the early generations of Arabs who worked with him in this field must go much of the credit for later developments in the Arab world. His military machine and the ambitious technical projects he envisaged may have been blighted by ignorance, but the seeds of the intellectual revolution which resulted from his more basic endeavors in education and translation have borne unanticipated fruit.

1. See J. Zaydān, *Ta'rīkh*, pp. 270–271. For an appreciation of the drastic style changes which have taken place, see the following specimens of early translated material in J. Tājir, *op. cit.*, pp. 135–153 and in A. Badawi, *op. cit.*, pp. 188–194. See also, I. M. Husaini, "Modern Arabic Literature," *Journal of World History*, Vol. III, No. 3, Paris: 1957, pp. 735–753.

FOUR

Arab Travellers to Europe

The translation into Arabic of books by European authors was only one symptom of the increased interest with which the Arabs of the early nineteenth century began to view the West. There were, at the same time, other contacts initiated between the two societies, contacts of a more personal nature which were to help the Arabs derive a fuller image of the West than was possible through reading translations of isolated books.

These personal contacts were of two kinds. First, more and more westerners were journeying to the Near East on military, commercial, and religious missions. These westerners were, in a sense, culture representatives, displaying by their actions and words the nature of their culture. Yet contact with these westerners could not help but be misleading since the Arabs tended to generalize from the few westerners they saw to the whole of western culture. This limitation was recognized early by the perceptive Lebanese encyclopaedist Butrus al-Bustāni, who warned his countrymen to beware of assuming that all Europeans were like "the lower class" representatives who had brought their vices to Lebanon or like the highly cultivated "upper class" Europeans whom he had met in Beirut. Neither group, he held, was typical of European society.[1]

The second type of contact was somewhat more rewarding because it was based upon a broader and more varied set of stimuli. Just as westerners had begun to travel to the Near East, so Arabs also journeyed westward for study, commercial enterprises, medical care, and diplomacy. Through such travel to Europe many Arabs gained

1. Buṭrus al-Bustāni, *Khiṭāb fi al-Hay'ah al-Ijtimā'iyah* (An Essay on Society), Beirut: 1869, pp. 38–40.

a first-hand impression and a more intimate knowledge of parts of the West. When these travellers returned, they tried, like all "tourists" to strange lands, to transmit their impressions to their friends and compatriots. Some spread their views among their immediate circle of friends only. This limited type of influence cannot be evaluated in terms of content or impact. Other travellers, although they did not record their impressions, had positions of influence and authority in their own countries. Through their policies they gave indirect knowledge to many. A third group of travellers, however, made their impact through the written word, recording their impressions of the West in published books that were widely circulated among literate Arabs both in their time and in later years. The contribution of this latter group to a more sophisticated image of the West was considerable and significant.

Pre-Nineteenth Century Travellers

Prior to the nineteenth century, Arab interest in the West was almost non-existent. As far as can be determined, between the fifteenth and the nineteenth centuries only one work appeared in Arabic which depicted the continent of Europe and that book was rather general and vague.

This does not mean that Arabs did not journey to Europe at all during that early period. To the contrary, we know of at least two significant trips during that era. The first was made by Fakhr al-Dīn al-Ma'ni, whose sojourn in Europe lasted the five years between 1613 and 1618. The second traveller was Ilyās Yuḥanna al-Mūṣili, whose trips to Europe and the New World covered a period of about fifteen years, between 1668 and 1683.

The record of the first traveller must be viewed through his subsequent activities, since he left no document which would indicate either his impressions of Italy or his understanding of European society. Despite the lack of a written record, there is little doubt that his trip affected him deeply. His subsequent attempts to change agricultural methods and architectural styles in Lebanon are lasting testaments to the effect of his western trip.[1]

The second traveller, however, described his trip in a short book subsequently entitled *Riḥlat Awwal Sharqi ila Amrīka* (The Trip of the First Oriental to America), published in 1906.[2] The book contained odd fragments of information of a geographical nature, chiefly about South America, and a few remarks about the people who inhabited that world. To what extent his original manuscript was known to his Arab contemporaries cannot be ascertained.

For our purposes, neither the subsequent behavior of Fakhr al-Dīn nor the treatise by al-Mūṣili can be considered significant influences in the transmission of European culture to the Arab world. Neither held up an image of the West which became consequential in or even incorporated into Arab developments.

Another type of Arab traveller to the West must be acknowledged. Toward the end of the seventeenth century, Maronite Christian students began to travel to Italy to study in the newly established theological seminary in Rome. Existing evidence indicates that these students were interested almost exclusively in religious matters and had little impact on other aspects of cultural development. They were trained theologians who subsequently returned to the Near East to practice their calling. A few remained in Italy and became "orientalists.". The writings of those who returned indicate few interests outside religion and, as far as can be determined, none of these theologians ever recorded his impressions of Europe. Whatever image they carried back with them may have been transmitted verbally through personal contact, but it is impossible to trace this.[3]

---

1. I. Ma'lūf, *Ta'rīkh al-Amīr Fakhr al-Dīn al-Ma'ni al-Thāni* (History of the Prince Fakhr al-Dīn the Second), Jūniyah: 1934, pp. 332–335; P. Paul Qara'li, *Fakhr al-Dīn* II, Vol. I, Harīṣah: 1937, pp. 137–155, Vol. II, 1938, pp. 263–315. It is apparent from these accounts that Fakhr al-Dīn's interest in Europe was rather limited and that, for the most part, his personal motives in maintaining close contacts with Europe were mainly to secure for himself a dynasty in the Lebanon. The exchange of correspondence between Fakhr al-Dīn and Italians indicates no other interests beside those of a technical nature.
2. E. Rabbath, ed., *Riḥlat Awwal Sharqi ila Amrīka*, by Yuḥanna al-Mūṣili, Beirut: 1906.
3. For short biographical notes on pre-nineteenth-century Lebanese who studied in the West, see Y. al-Dibs, *Mukhtaṣar Ta'rīkh Sūrīyah* (A Short History of Syria),

Nineteenth-Century Travellers

The important period of contact with the West through travel commenced at the beginning of the nineteenth century. We have already referred to the student missions which Muḥammad 'Ali and subsequent Viceroys of Egypt sent to Europe.[1] These missions were important in two ways. First, the students returned with an image of Europe which they translated into reality through their activities on the bureaucratic level. And second, they spread information about Europe to those with whom they came in personal contact. However, only one of these students left any record of his years of residence in Europe. This exception was al-Shaykh Rifā'ah Rāfi' al-Ṭahṭāwi, whose importance in Arab affairs as a translator has already been noted and to whose travel memoirs we will return in a later section of this chapter.

The nineteenth-century influx of Arabs into Europe was not confined to these student missions, however. The closer Europe came to the Arab world through military and commercial expansion, the more aware the Arabs became of the former's importance and promise. Thus, Near Easterners began to travel to Europe for study, for medical treatment, or for business transactions. Still later, other Arabs were to travel on official missions or to conduct diplomatic relations. By the end of the nineteenth century this growing number of Arabs in Europe was supplemented by the exiles from Ḥamīdian oppression in the Levant.

Many of these travellers made extremely important contributions to the literary or political life of the Arab world. While most of the individuals who had been to Europe manifested the results of their trip in their behavior, some of them contributed more lastingly by writing about what they had actually seen during their visits. Their recorded impressions are, therefore, basic to an understanding of

---

Beirut: 1907, Vol. II, pp. 199–204, 259–268. See also P. K. Hitti, *History of Syria*, New York: 1951, pp. 675–676, and his *Lebanon in History*, New York: 1957, pp. 398–407.

1. See pp. 50–51 above.

their cultural and political outlook – an outlook which they communicated to their compatriots through their books.

This chapter investigates the more important travellers, and describes the nature of their works and the motivations which impelled them to publish their impressions. Succeeding chapters summarize their major observations about European society and life.

As might be expected, the travellers who actually recorded their impressions were but a small minority of all those who ventured abroad. However, the influence of that minority far outweighs its numerical weakness. These men constituted an important part of the intellectual leadership in the nineteenth-century Arab milieu. Some of them directly influenced the course of Arab history during their lifetimes, and practically all of them were widely read by the literate public of the Arab Near East. Therefore, the ideas they disseminated as well as the courses of action they followed are crucial to any inquiry into the nascent Arab awareness of the West.

One example indicative of the degree to which Europe influenced a major figure of nineteenth-century Arabic literature might be cited. Mārūn al-Naqqāsh (1817–1855), who is credited with being the father of Arabic drama, journeyed to Italy as a young man. There he saw for the first time a play performed on the stage. In a later book he described the observations which had so significant an effect upon his subsequent writings:

> When I passed through the European countries ... I saw the theaters which are a means designed to cultivate and improve the nature of man. There [in the theaters] they perform strange acts and tell wondrous stories ... These plays and stories have a double nature. On the surface they are witty and filled with allusions. Underneath, there is a great deal of Good and Truth in them ... Even the Kings are attracted by their wisdom and leave their thrones in order to view them ... These theaters are divided into two distinct types ... The first is known as The *Brūzah* [Prose] and the second is called the *Ūberah* [Opera]. The *Brūzah* in turn is divided into *Kumedia* and *Trajidya.* All of these are acted with simple prose and without accompaniment of music. The *Ūberah* is similarly divided into sad and happy ... The first type [*Brūzah*] is more important and compelling to analyze and render into

> Arabic because it is the simpler and more intimate of the two. As an introduction, therefore, it is more appropriate ...[1]

Immediately upon his return he wrote and produced the first Arabic play "on stage." The play form was well received and has continued to flourish as an accepted art in the Arab world.

Nineteenth-Century Travel Accounts

A roster of all Arabs who travelled to Europe during the nineteenth century cannot be compiled, nor would it serve much purpose. On the other hand, a list of those Arabs who published accounts of their journeys is both possible and significant. The content of these books will be analyzed later, but the following list is presented here to give the reader an overall impression of chronology, important writers, and their works.[2]

1834 R. R. Ṭahṭāwi, *Takhlīṣ al-Ibrīz ila Talkhīṣ Bārīz* (The Extraction of Gold in the Summary of Paris), First Imprint Cairo, 1834. Reprinted in 1848, 1905, and 1958, 262 pages. An account based on his stay in France between 1826–1831.[3]

---

1. Mārūn al-Naqqāsh, *Arzat Lubnān* (The Cedar of Lebanon), Beirut: 1896, pp. 15–16. See also, N. Barbour, "The Arabic Theatre in Egypt," in *BSOS*, Vol. VIII, Part I, London: 1935, pp. 173–187, and Part IV, 1937, pp. 991–1012; and J. Landau, *Studies in the Arab Theater and Cinema*, Philadelphia: 1958, pp. 57–61.

2. This list does not include travel accounts of Andalusia, geographically a part of Europe. These accounts were written by North African Arabs in the eighteenth and nineteenth centuries who journeyed to southern Spain for "sentimental" reasons. For information and an analysis of their works see Henri Pérès, *L'Espagne vue par les voyageurs Musulmans de* 1610 *à* 1930, Paris: 1937. See also the bibliographic article of Pérès, "Voyageurs Musulmans en Europe aux XIXe et XXe siécles," in *Mémoires de l'Institut Français d' Archéologie Orientale du Caire*, Vol. LXVIII, Cairo: 1940, pp. 185–195.

3. See Shaykhu, *al-Ādāb al-'Arabīyah fi al-Qarn al-Tāsi' 'Ashar*, Vol. II, pp. 8 ff.; Sarkīs, *Mu'jam al-Matbū'āt al-'Arabīyah wa al-Mu'rrabah*, Cairo: 1928, p. 942; Zaydān, *Ta'rīkh*, p. 296, and his *Mashāhīr*, Vol. II, pp. 19 ff.; C. Huart, *Littérature Arabe*, Paris: 1912, pp. 406–407; Carra de Vaux, *Penseurs de l'Islam*, Vol. v, Paris: 1926, pp. 235–244; *Encyclopedia of Islam*, Vol. III, 1924, pp. 1155–1156; C. Brockelmann, *Geschichte der Arabischen Litteratur*, Leipzig: 1902, Vol. II, 1938,

1855 Aḥmad Fāris al-Shidyāq, *al-Sāq 'Ala al-Sāq fi Māhuwa al-Fāryāq* (La vie et les aventures de Fariac), published originally in Paris, 1855, and reprinted in Cairo in 1919 and 1920. Only portions of this work deal with France and England.[1]

1856 Salīm Bustrus, *al-Nuzah al-Shahīyah fi al-Riḥlah al-Salīmīyah* (The Delightful Excursion of Salim), Beirut, 1856. 132 pp. Based on his observations of Italy, France, England, Belgium, and other countries which he had visited one year previously.[2]

1866 Aḥmad Fāris al-Shidyāq, *Kashf al-Mukhabba' 'an Funūn Ūrubba*(Unveiling the Arts of Europe), printed originally in Tunis in 1866 and reprinted in Constantinople in 1881. The latter edition includes an earlier work on Malta. 361 pages, 67 of which deal with Malta. This and his earlier book noted above were based on his observations in England and France between 1848 and 1852.

1867 Fransīs Marrāsh, *Riḥlah ila Ūrubba* (A Trip to Europe), Beirut, 1867. 72 pages. Based on his second journey to Europe in 1866.[3]

1867 Sulaymān al Ḥarāyri, *'Arḍ al-Baḍā'i' al-'āmm* (Exposition Universelle, 1866), Paris, 1867. An account of his impressions of the Parisian trade fair held in 1866.[4]

1867 Khayr al-Dīn al-Tūnisi, *Aqwām al-Masālik fi Ma'rifat Aḥwāl al-Mamālik* (The Best Paths to the Knowledge of

p. 731; J. Heyworth-Dunne, "Rifā'ah," *BSOS*, Vol. IX, 1939, pp. 961–967; and A. Dāghir, *Maṣādir al-Dirāsah al-Adabīyah*, Beirut: 1955, pp. 569–574.

1. Shaykhu, *op. cit.*, Vol. I, pp. 86–87; Sarkīs, *op. cit.*, pp. 1104–1108; Zaydān, *Ta'rīkh*, Vol. IV, pp. 225 ff.; and his *Mashāhīr*, Vol. II, pp. 81 ff.; *Encyclopedia of Islam*, Vol. I, 1908, pp. 67–88; Brockelmann, *op. cit.*, Vol. II, p. 867; A. Dāghir, *op. cit.*, pp. 471–478; and M. A. Khalafallah, *Aḥmad Fāris al-Shidyāq*, Cairo: 1955.

2. Shaykhu, *op. cit.*, Vol. II, p. 113; Sarkīs, *op. cit.*, p. 563; Zaydān, *Mashāhīr*, pp. 145–148; and C. Brockelmann, *op. cit.*, Vol. II, p. 757.

3. Shaykhu, *op. cit.*, Vol. II, pp. 41–43; Sarkīs, *op. cit.*, p. 1730; Zaydān, *Mashāhīr*. Vol. II, pp. 253–257; M. R. Ṭabbākh, *A'lām al-Nubalā'bi Ta'rīkh Ḥalab* (The Notables in the History of Aleppo), Aleppo: 1929, pp. 363–368; Brockelmann, *op. cit.*, Vol. II, pp. 755–756; and A. Dāghir, *op. cit.*, pp. 693–697.

4. Shaykhu, *op. cit.*, Vol. II, p. 60. Sarkīs, *op. cit.*, p. 747.

the Realms), first published in Tunis in 1867 and reprinted in Alexandria in 1881. 467 pages. Based on several trips he made to Europe between 1850 and 1865.[1]

1874 Luwīs Ṣābunji, *al-Riḥlah al-Naḥlīyah*. (The Trip of the Bee), published in Constantinople in 1874. Based on his world trip between 1871 and 1874.[2]

1874 Muḥammad Bayram (5th) *Ṣafwat al-I'tibār bi Mustawda' al-Amṣār wa al-Aqṭār* (The Purest Consideration in the Location of Countries), published in 5 volumes in Cairo between 1884 and 1886. The total work is about 1,000 pages, but only three of the five volumes deal with Europe. The remainder describe his travels in the Islamic World, particularly in North Africa. Based on his numerous trips to Europe which commenced in 1867.[3]

1876 Nakhlah Ṣāleḥ, *al-Kanz al-Mukhabba' li al-Siyāḥah fi Ūrubba* (The Hidden Treasures in a Trip to Europe). Based on his impressions of various European countries which he visited in 1875.[4]

1888 Muḥammad Sharīf Salīm, *Riḥlah ila Ūrubba* (A Trip to Europe), published in Cairo in 1888. 82 pages. Based on his sojourn in France when he was teaching Arabic in Paris.[5]

1891 Dimitri Khilāṭ, *Sifr al-Safar ila Ma'raḍ al-Ḥaḍar* (The Book of Travel to the Exhibition of the Civilized), published in Cairo in 1891. 282 pages. Based on his

1. Shaykhu, *op. cit.*, Vol. II, pp. 25 ff.; Sarkīs, *op. cit.*, p. 854; Zaydān, *Ta'rīkh*, Vol. IV, p. 290; Aḥmad Amīn, *Zu'amā' al-Iṣlāḥ fi al-'Aṣr al-Ḥadīth* (Leaders of Reform in the Modern Era), Cairo: 1948, pp. 164 ff.; Brockelmann, *op. cit.*, Vol. II, p. 887; and Dāghir, *op. cit.*, pp. 226–229.

2. Sarkīs, *op. cit.*, p. 1177; *P. Tarrāzi, Ta'rīkh al-Ṣaḥāfah al-'Arabīyah*, Beirut: 1913, 1914, and 1923, Vol. II, pp. 47, 52.

3. Shaykhu, *op. cit.*, Vol. II. p. 112; Sarkīs, *op. cit.*, p. 614; Zaydān, *Mashāhīr*. Vol. II, pp. 241 ff. and his *Ta'rīkh*, Vol. IV, p. 289; C. Van Dyke, *Iktifā' al-Qanū' fi Māhuwa Matbū'*, p. 414; *Encyclopedia of Islam*, Vol. III, 1924, pp. 684–686.

4. Sarkīs, *op. cit.*, p. 1189.

5. *Ibid.*, p. 1656.

observations while travelling in Europe for the main purpose of attending the Parisian Trade Fair of 1890.[1]

1891 Ḥasan Tawfiq, *Rasā'il al-Bushra fi al-Siyāḥah bi Almānya wa Swīsra* (Glad Tidings in the Journey to Germany and Switzerland), published in Cairo, 1891. 55 pages. Based on his observations of those two countries in the summer of 1890. He was teaching Arabic in Berlin.[2]

1891 Muḥammad al-Tūnisi al-Sanūsi, *al-Istiṭla'āt al-Bārīsīyah* (Parisian Curiosities), published in Tunis in 1891. 279 pages. Based on his sojourn in France to attend the Parisian Trade Fair of 1890.[3]

1891 Maḥmūd 'Umar al-Bājūri, *al-Durar al-Bahīyah fi al-Riḥlah al-Ūrubbāwīyah* (The Beautiful Gems in a Trip to Europe), published in Cairo. 96 pages. Depicts his impressions of Europe which he visited to attend the Eighth International Congress of Orientalists held in Stockholm in 1889.[4]

1892 Amīn Fikri, *Irshād al-Alibbā' ila Maḥāsin Ūrubba* (The Intelligent Man's Guide to the Beauties of Europe), Cairo, 1892. 821 pages. Based on his travels through Europe to attend the Orientalists' Congress in Stockholm in 1889. The work was published posthumously.[5]

1893 Aḥmad Zaki, *al-Safar ila al-Mu'tamar* (The Journey to the Conference), published in Cairo in 1893. 400 pages. His impressions while *en route* to the Ninth Orientalists' Conference in London during that same year.

1893 Khalīl Sarkīs, *Riḥlat Mudīr al-Lisān ila al-āsitānah wa Ūrubba wa Amrīka* (The Journey of the Director [Khalīl Sarkīs] to Constantinople, Europe, and America). Published in Cairo, 1893. 141 pages. Based on his trip in 1892 to those countries.[6]

---

1. *Ibid.*, p. 832.
2. *Ibid.*, p. 756.
3. *Ibid.*, p. 1057.
4. Sarkīs, *Ibid.*, p. 511.
5. Zaydān, *Mashāhīr*, pp. 272–278 and his *Ta'rīkh*, Vol. IV, pp. 241–242; Shaykhu, *op. cit.*, pp. 95–96, 98–100.
6. Sarkīs, *op. cit.*, p. 1020.

1900 'Ali Abū al-Futūḥ, *Siyāḥat Miṣri fi Ūrubba* (The Travel of an Egyptian in Europe), Cairo, 1900. 88 pages. His impressions of France and Italy which he visited in the same year.[1]

1900 Aḥmad Zaki, *al-Dunya fi Bārīs* (Life in Paris), published in Cairo in 1900. 272 pages. Based on his trip to France in 1899.[2]

The eighteen travellers who recorded their impressions of Europe during the nineteenth century are, to our knowledge, the only ones whose books were published. There is a great possibility that other works were prepared in manuscript form but never reached publication. A case in point is the work of Ibrāhīm al-Najjār, who travelled to Europe in 1856. The publication of his book on Europe was announced, but it never appeared in print.[3] It is unlikely that this was an isolated case.

Of the eighteen travellers, six made their trips prior to 1870. Of these, three were Syrian, two Tunisian, and one Egyptian. Three of them were sent on official missions. After 1870, the situation differs somewhat. Of the remaining twelve, seven were Egyptian, three were Syrian, and two were Tunisian. Only two of this later group had been sent on official missions. The majority of the travellers were Muslims.

The number of works produced during each period may also indicate the growing importance of Europe to the Arab world. During the first seven decades of the nineteenth century, the number of travellers was rather limited, and this was reflected in the small number of books written about Europe in that interval. Prior to 1850 only one

1. *Ibid.*, p. 332.

2. Sarkīs, *Ibid.*, p. 971; "Aḥmad Zaki," in *al-Muqtaṭaf*, Vol. 84, Cairo: 1934, pp 153 ff.; "Aḥmad Zaki, " in *al-Hilāl*, Vol. 42, Cairo: 1933, pp. 1173 ff.; and Dāghir, *op. cit.*, pp. 422–426.

3. al-Najjār, in his *Miṣbāḥ al-Sāri wa Nuzhat al-Qāri'* (The Traveller's Lamp and the Delight of the Reader), published in Beirut in 1858, wrote in the introduction: "I have divided my work into two volumes. The first contains my trip to Egypt … and Constantinople … The second contains … my trip to Europe."(p. 2)

No publishers' records or bibliographers' lists indicate that this second volume existed and we may assume that it was never published. Pérès, in the bibliographical article, mentions a few titles of manuscripts of travel accounts which were not published.

author had published his impressions. In the 1850s, two more books appeared. Four books appeared in the 1860s. By this date both interest in Europe and travel to her shores had increased substantially. After 1870 many important Arab political and literary figures made the "pilgrimage" to Europe and, in the short span of thirty years, no less than fourteen books of travel appeared.[1]

The Subject Matter of the Travel Books

The general classification of these books as travel accounts does not mean that they were, therefore, similar to each other in subject matter or even approach. Although the books had in common a preoccupation with geographic descriptions of the places visited by the authors, there the resemblance ends. The differences between the books must be explained in terms of both the dates when they were written (earlier books required more elementary and background information while later books could assume a certain amount of knowledge on the part of the reader) and the interests and predilections of the individual authors.

Since Ṭahṭāwi was one of the first Egyptians to travel to Europe in the nineteenth century and the first, to our knowledge, to publish a book about that unknown area,[2] to him fell the most difficult task of serving as Arab ethnographer to a "strange land with strange

1. At the turn of the century, books were being printed at so fast a rate that it is difficult to make the arbitrary division between nineteenth and twentieth century. For example, the travels of Muḥammad Farīd, Muḥammad 'Ali, and M. Labīb al-Batanūni, all Egyptians, which took place in 1900, have been excluded from our list because their books were not published until 1901. The works on the West published during the first half of the twentieth century total almost four times the number written during the entire nineteenth century. See the listings of Sarkīs, *op. cit.*, pp. 332, 418, 525, 832, 1192, 1300, 1549, 1657, 1682, and 1686; of Dāghir, *op. cit.*, pp. 294, 340, and 657; and Pérès, "Voyageurs," pp. 188–195, for illustrations of the changes in numerical composition.

2. Ṭahṭāwi himself made the claim of being the first in his *Takhlīṣ*, p. 4, and this claim has never been disputed. His work has more than superficial resemblance to early anthropological studies of primitive societies by westerners. Because his readers were presumed to be entirely ignorant, he devoted considerable space to terminology, artifacts, and ritualistic behavior. For example, he describes the clothing of Europeans, their houses, their carriages, and their dancing.

customs." This task he performed in competent if somewhat eclectic and unsystematic fashion. He introduced his readers slowly and carefully to the minutiae of culture by giving (a) a transliteration of each European term for which no Arabic substitute was available, (b) a lesson in how the word was to be pronounced, and (c) a detailed and literal description of its physical properties or its sequence of actions. Samples of the new elements of western culture which he introduced to his readers will be given in a later section.[1] Similar details had to be given concerning the geographic location of the places mentioned and their physical characteristics. These elements in Ṭahṭāwi's book seem to have been dictated by the time at which he wrote.

Other elements, however, were more akin to his natural interests in politics and education. Thus, his book included a fairly complete description of the basic political organization of France, which he had visited. In addition, he discussed the state and nature of learning in Europe and introduced his readers to some of the authors and outstanding European intellectual works on society and literature.

Ṭahṭāwi's book, therefore, gave a crucial introduction to the hitherto mysterious European world and culture. However, if any theme predominated in his book which could be used to characterize it, it was his emphasis on the political-educational aspect of France.

In contrast to this, the later works of Shidyāq were almost exclusively concerned with the social structure of England and France. They included, of course, geographic information on the towns and cities he had visited, but, on the whole, it was French and English society that most concerned him. Almost no attention was paid to the political systems in either country. What Ṭahṭāwi had done to familiarize Arab readers with French customs, Shidyāq did to introduce their English equivalents. Shidyāq's books also set an important precedent for later travellers by including historical information.[2]

The work of Salīm Bustrus is primarily a descriptive account of the various European countries he visited and contains almost a tourist guide-book treatment of the European cities he had seen. Manners

1. See Chapters V and VI.

2. Khayr al-Dīn and Muḥammad Bayram followed this precedent most noticeably, but other authors as well began to include historical background in their studies.

and customs, artifacts and "novel" aspects of European material culture are presented in detail. The items selected for description shed light on what an Arab of that period saw as novel by contrast. The state of learning in Europe receives indirect appraisal, since Bustrus includes in his discussion informative statistics on libraries and museums, their holdings, and their users.

Fransis Marrāsh's book is much briefer but in many ways more sophisticated. He, too, was concerned chiefly with describing the French towns he had seen, particularly Paris, which fascinated him as it had his predecessors and would his successors. The major significance of the book, however, lies in what it conveyed concerning the educational progress in France. Marrāsh was deeply impressed by the value that the French people attached to learning *per se* and by the role that reason and liberty played in the integration of society.

Ḥarāyrī's pamphlet, though limited in scope, included fresh information about the material culture of Europe. It dealt specifically with the trade fair held in Paris in 1866, its physical setting, its organization and sections, and the artifacts displayed.

Perhaps the most comprehensive view of Europe presented by the early travellers appeared in the work of Khayr al-Dīn al-Tūnisi.[1] In terms of organization and scope, his monumental study was a landmark in the transmission of knowledge about the West. The work was divided, following the manner of Ibn Khaldūn, into two parts. The first part he called the *Muqaddimah* (prolegomena), in which he constructed a comparative image of European and Islamic societies. His purpose was to explore the basic causes of Europe's progress and Islam's decline and to offer remedies for the latter's decadence. In the narration of this first part, information on the development of European society and on the evolution of scientific knowledge in Europe was also presented. The second part was devoted to a description of each European country, giving geographic characteristics, inform ation about population size and distribution, and facts concerning

1. Khayr al-Dīn al-Tūnisi, *Aqwām al-Masālik fī Ma'rifat Aḥwāl al-Mamālik*, Tunis: 1867.

political organization and military strength. He prefaced each description with an historical introduction to the country's past.

A few remarks concerning the books published after 1870 may be ventured here, although details of these later works are somewhat out of place. Of the twelve travellers who published studies between 1870 and 1900, perhaps the most significant were Muḥammad Bayram, Aḥmad Zaki, and Muḥammad al-Tūnisi. The former, who evidently followed the lead of his fellow countryman, Khayr al-Dīn, wrote a five-volume geopolitical analysis of Italy, France, and England. Historical and geographical information was presented for each country and, in addition, descriptions were given of the political system, the state of education, the nature of the economy – imports, exports, agricultural products, etc. – and health and recreational facilities. Some information was also included on the customs and manners of the people.

The latter two authors were more concerned with the daily life of Europeans. Their works paralleled Shidyāq's more closely than they resembled either the eclectic observations of Ṭahṭāwi, the specificity and limited scope of Ḥarāyri, the geographic pre-occupation of Marrāsh and Bustrus, or the historical breadth of Khayr al-Dīn.

The remaining authors of the nineteenth century were primarily concerned with physical descriptions of European places and objects; only passing mention is made of political institutions or intellectual developments.

Impact of the Travels

The travels to Europe by the six pre-1870 authors had a two-fold impact. First, their travels affected them directly, and they applied many of the things they had witnessed abroad to their own fields when they returned. Second, their travels affected others indirectly by providing them with a vicarious stimulus.

Of course, it is almost impossible to measure with any accuracy the weight of either impact. However, we do have evidence to indicate that the trips did affect the subsequent behavior of the travellers and that their books were sufficiently widely read to influence a large sector of the reading public, including the authors of later travel books.

The above list of volumes shows that the works of Ṭahṭāwi, Shidyāq, and Khayr al-Dīn were all printed more than once. This would indicate a certain sustained interest in the books, even though the exact number of copies in circulation cannot be ascertained. In addition, the educated elite who read these books was assumed to have a familiarity with the literature and, in fact, the authors themselves made numerous references to works which preceded their own. For example, Shidyāq referred his readers to Ṭahṭāwi's book for a fuller description of Paris.[1] Khayr al-Dīn also referred to Ṭahṭawi's book in connection with the state of learning in France.[2] Muḥammad Bayram called the attention of his readers to the works of Ṭahṭāwi, Shidyāq, and Khayr al-Dīn for supporting evidence or more complete descriptions.[3]

Not only were educated readers presumably familiar with these works but they also gave great credence to statements which appeared in them, because of the authority of the authors. This was evidently true as late as 1920 if the following story recounted by a western observer is accepted:

> The Musulman students in Cairo, Stanboul, and even distant Samarkand, have acquired their knowledge of European peoples and manners and customs from the writings of this man, Aḥmad Faris [Shidyāq] Effendi, and his *Kashf al-Mukhabba.*
>
> Not very long ago I was conversing with a teacher in the El Azhar University (Cairo) about the legendary plagues of Egypt and diseases in general. He solemnly informed me that the most efficient cure for epilepsy is to swallow a live rat or frog; adding that it was a well-known European remedy, as I could see for myself in the *Kashf al-Mukhabba* of the learned Faris Effendi. When I said that although I admired the works of this author very much, yet I did not quite agree with many of his statements, my Egyptian friend became quite indignant, asking, with true

1. Shidyāq, *Kashf*, pp. 222, 289.
2. Khayr al-Dīn, *op. cit.*, p. 69.
3. M. Bayram, *Ṣafwat al-I'tibār bi Mustawda' al-Amṣār wa al-Aqṭār*, Cairo: 1884–1886, Vol. IV, pp. 56–57.

> Oriental logic, "Do you mean to say that you doubt the word of the great scholar whom you got to translate your own Holy Book? You are like the rest of your countrymen, who only believe what they wish to believe, and reject what is unpleasant to their feelings. What Faris Effendi says about your country is the truth, and that is why you do not believe him."[1]

We can suggest certain reasons why these works should have been trusted so completely. First, the writers were prominent and respected figures in the fields of politics and the arts. They were admired, not only for their writings but for their activities as well. Second, their books were written in a highly cultivated and traditional style filled with Islamic allusions and proverbs. And third, most of the Muslim writers had been trained in theology and therefore belonged to the '*Ulamā*' class. All three factors would have predisposed their audiences to accept what they read.

We might return now to the first point, that the men themselves were deeply affected by their travels and translated much of what they had learned into practical behavior. One way of demonstrating this is to show relationships between the subsequent actions of these authors and the things they observed in Europe. Ṭahṭāwi, it will be remembered, became director of the School of Languages in Cairo after his return from Europe. It has been suggested[2] that he patterned that institution after the School of Oriental Languages in Paris, which was then under the direction of Sylvestre de Sacy. It is known that Ṭahṭāwi was on friendly terms with the latter and had great respect for his ability and competence. In fact, he submitted his manuscript of *Takhlī ṣ* to de Sacy for criticisms and comments before permitting its publication. There can be little doubt that Ṭahṭāwi's observations of the School of Oriental Languages suggested to him at least the broad outlines of the Egyptian school he directed.

Salīm Bustrus and Fransīs Marrāsh were, in a literary way,

---

1. Fitzgerald Lee, "An Arab Journalist on England," *National Review*, Vol. LXXV, London: 1920, p. 379. It must be noted that the alleged "cure" is nowhere mentioned in Shidyāq's books.
2. See Aḥmad Amīn, *Fayḍ al-Khāṭir* (Reflections), Vol. V, Cairo: 1948, p. 87. For more direct evidence, see Ṭahṭāwi himself in *Takhlīṣ*, pp. 179–183.

similarly affected by their contact with France. The former concentrated his later activities on translation of novels, evidently because he believed they were worthy of attention.[1] His activities in this direction, however, were limited by the demands of his business. Fransīs Marrāsh, on the other hand, reacted in a somewhat different manner. Although he did not translate French books, his entire literary approach was shaped by the influence of French literature. After his return to Aleppo he wrote the first "political" novel to appear in modern Arabic literature. Throughout his works the themes of liberty, equality, and social justice are constantly evident.[2]

Perhaps Khayr al-Dīn was the traveller most aware of his own desire to emulate what he had seen in the West. A statesman and administrator before his departure to Europe, he carried with him a great interest in the political aspects of Europe. Upon his return, he exerted great efforts to create similar political institutions in his own country. With conscious acknowledgments and unequivocal value judgments, Khayr al-Dīn referred to his suggestions as reforms (*Iṣlāḥāt* and *Tanzīmāt*) based upon the European model.

M. Bayram was similarly affected by European political institutions, especially those relating to civil rights. He also was active politically until he was finally exiled from Tunis by the French. Prior to his exile, he occupied important administrative posts and was directly responsible for the reorganization of hospitals, for the *Awqāf*, and for reforms in the educational system. All of these activities occurred after his trip to Europe where he studied parallel European institutions.[3]

Two facts are evident in the narration thus far. On the one hand, it is suggested that nineteenth-century Arab travellers played an important role in shaping the emerging image of the West despite their small numbers. On the other hand, their very existence suggests a major shift in the world-focus of the Arabs.

1. See for example his translation of *The Wonders of Fate* by Adolph Philo, which appeared as *Gharā'ib al-Aqdār*. Second edition, 1890.
2. His first novel was entitled *Ghābat al-Ḥaqq* (The Forest of Truth), Beirut: 1866. For comments on his role as an innovator, see R. Khūri, *al-Fikr al-'Arabi al-Ḥadīth*, Beirut: 1943, pp. 187–188 and P. K. Hitti, "The Impact of the West on Syria and Lebanon in the Nineteenth Century," *loc. cit.*, p. 628.
3. Zaydān, *Mashāhīr*, p. 215; *Encyclopedia of Islam*, Vol. III, 1924, p. 685.

The number of Arabs sojourning in Europe increased throughout the nineteenth century. That in itself is a critical fact. But that some Arabs should record their impressions is perhaps even more significant. Prior to the nineteenth century, Arabs had taken little or no interest in Europe; their main interest was in the Muslim countries of the Orient. While prior to the nineteenth century, Arab geographers and travellers exhibited an unusual lack of information about western Europe – a fact not unrelated to their lack of interest in that area – Arab travellers of the nineteenth century attempted to rectify the situation. They began to supply accurate, if elementary, data about the West as well as they could under the circumstances.

Commensurate with the increase in travel to Europe was a decline in travel to Eastern realms.[1] While this decline may not be significant in itself, when taken in the context of the self-centeredness of the Arabs of previous decades, it does reflect a waning interest in the Arab world and an increasing interest in the "rising" (as they viewed it) continent of Europe.

This shift was clear in practically all facets of Arab development in the nineteenth century. In increasing numbers students chose or were sent to Europe for education instead of to Constantinople or to local institutions of higher learning. Similarly, missionary schools began to attract students across religious lines more than they had previously. Finally, Arab intellectual leaders chose, almost without exception, European exile, particularly in France, during the oppressive regimes in the Arab world.[2] All these indicate a growth in Arab awareness of the West which was to have an important effect on Arab intellectual evolution.

The importance of the early travellers and especially of those travellers who published books about Europe, then, becomes even greater when it is viewed within the context of an entire movement. During the nineteenth century, these books were one of the very few

1. Sarkīs, *op. cit.*, pp. 19, 1291, 1456, 1663, 1682, can be referred to for an impression of the decline in relative importance of travel to other Muslim lands during that era.

2. Among some of the more influential of these, we might mention Muḥammad 'Abduh, Adīb Isḥāq, the famed Abū Nazzārah (James Sanū), Fatḥi Zaghlūl, and M. Kāmel.

means which were available to the literate population for gaining an understanding of Europe and for constructing their first image of the West. Much of what the authors wrote was absorbed by Arab intellectuals whose familiarity with the West was shaped by these early impressions and whose later knowledge was colored by them.

FIVE

Travellers' Views of Europe: Political and Social Organization

The Arabs of the nineteenth century formed their first blurred image of the West on the basis of information provided by Arab travellers to Europe. The identity of these travellers has already been established, but the content of their works remains to be explored. This and the following chapters describe some of the ideas, impressions, and reactions which appear in the travel books – and for no idle purpose. Much of what the travellers wrote ultimately drifted into the mainstream of Arab cultural awareness. For this reason, the content of their works and the attitudes underlying their approach take on especial significance.

Not only the content of the volumes but also the principles which guided the selection of items for inclusion are indicative of the level of cultural perception. The latter is often a sensitive indirect index to the travellers' values and capacities to comprehend. What a traveller fails to observe may sometimes be as important as what he actually does perceive in a foreign culture. Thus, an analysis of the sources requires a study not only of what items were covered but also what important elements of European life received little or no attention.

The selection of certain phenomena of European life for detailed discussion by the travellers may indicate one of several things. It may indicate a prior sensitivity to these phenomena on the part of the observer, a sensitivity which endowed the phenomena with intrinsic interest, even in the absence of utilitarian purpose. Or a phenomenon may commend itself to the attention of the observer because the observer makes invidious comparisons between his own culture and the new one, wishing either to emulate the new culture or to justify his own. Finally, it may indicate that a phenomenon in the foreign culture is perceived to be so bizarre as to warrant special attention, either to amuse the reader or to discredit its cultural meaning.

Similarly, the failure of a writer to include a discussion of other parts of the culture may indicate either that he failed to perceive these phenomena or that he took it for granted that his readers were completely familiar with them. It may also mean, however, that the phenomena were so subtle that an outsider could not fully understand their significance. These selective principles are all found, to some extent, in the writings of the Arab travellers.

In the following sections, an ordering of topics has been introduced which is not to be found in the original travel manuscripts. In the latter, observations on the political system, for example, are interspersed with reflections on scenery, comments on means of transportation, and descriptions of dress and manners. Such a pattern of organization was not uncommon in Arabic literature at that time, although it introduces inconveniences for the contemporary analyst.

The Political Organization of the State

References to the political aspects of Europe in pre-1870 writings of Arab travellers are to be found chiefly in the works of Ṭahṭāwi, Fransīs Marrāsh, and Khayr al-Dīn. There are also occasional comments made by Shidyāq, but these are less significant. Among the works published between 1870 and 1900, the books of Muḥammad Bayram contain the most detailed political comments; only minor remarks are to be found in the works of other contemporary writers.

It should be pointed out that, although pre-1870 writers often generalized their political observations to "Europe," in reality they had specific knowledge only of the French political system. Only Khayr al-Dīn mentioned that other European countries were not the same as France and specifically warned his readers not to include the two tyrannical states of the Vatican and Russia among the states whose political organization he described.

Perhaps the most important aspect of political organization

noted by the travellers was the European principle of a government of laws, rather than of men. To state the observation briefly, they noted that the distinguishing characteristic of European government was its "constitutionalism" – regardless of whether it was republican or monarchical. It was also noted that there were very explicit distinctions made between the various branches of government, i.e., the principle of the separation of powers. Ṭahṭāwi, for example, described the French system in the following manner:

> Let us elucidate the way in which the French conduct their affairs [of state] ... so that their conduct may serve as a lesson from which to learn. We have stated that Paris is the Capital of the French; there the French monarch and his family reside. The French monarch is of the Bourbon family since he cannot be from any other family. The French monarchy is an hereditary one. The place where the monarch lives is called the Tuilleries [pronunciation given] and generally the French refer to their *Dīwān* [Cabinet] as the Tuilleries Cabinet ... that is, the *Dīwān* of the monarch. The real seat of power in the direction of French affairs is the king, but secondary power resides in the Upper House, which is the *Dīwān* of the *Bīr* [transliteration of *Paris*] ... and the Chamber of Deputies ... [A lengthy statement follows here describing the various Dīwāns or ministries.]
>
> Therefore, the French monarch is the possessor of great powers, *provided* he acts in accordance with the desires of the aforementioned assemblies ... He has specific powers which will be mentioned in our discussion of French politics.
>
> The duty of the Upper House is the renewal of laws which have expired and the maintenance of the existing law. Also it is expected that this assembly will support the monarch in his rights, defend him, and steadfastly reject those who oppose the monarchy. This assembly is convened by the king for a specified period during the year, to correspond with the session of the Chamber of Deputies ... The duty of the Chamber of Deputies is the examination of laws, policies and orders of the government and its management of the country's affairs. It also discusses the budget of the state, its revenues and expenditures, and opposes measures which it does not deem wise. It also defends the rights of the people, so that no injustice or transgression can take place. This assembly is composed of many men who are elected to office by the people. There are 428 deputies; they cannot serve unless

they are at least forty years old. Each member must, in addition, possess property, the income from which must be at least 1000 francs a year.

The ministers of the state are many ... [these are enumerated here together with their functions].

From this it is apparent that the French monarch is not an absolute ruler who can do what he wishes. French policy is a written law so that the ruler can remain king only if he acts in accordance with what is prescribed in the laws which have met with the acceptance of the members of the various assemblies. While the Upper House defends the King, the Chamber of Deputies protects the rights of the people ...

Since it is impossible for all the people to participate in the management of the state, the people delegate the work to 430 deputies who are sent to Paris for consultation. These delegates are selected by the people and are authorized by them to defend their rights and to act in the best interest of the people. Each Frenchman who is eligible – one of the conditions for eligibility is that the person be at least twenty-five years old – has the right to participate in the election of his deputies. Each Frenchman can also be a deputy, provided he has reached thirty-five years of age, and provided that his other qualifications conform to the conditions prescribed by law ... [A statement on the number of deputies from each district is included here.] Each elector writes his choice on a piece of paper and gives it in turn to the responsible man in the election station who in turn places this paper in the ballot box.

The Chamber of Deputies is elected for a five-year term, after which a new election takes place. No election can take place without the approval of the two chambers and the king. The people of the towns [constituents] can communicate with their representatives by means of petitions if they wish to complain about any matter or if they wish to propose a useful program.[1]

Other remarks on French politics by this same author are closely tied to his analysis of the French Revolution and its achievements. Ṭahṭāwi recounted how the French people arose in rebellion (in

1. Ṭahṭāwi, *Takhlīṣ*, pp. 79–81. Between 1815 and 1831, French electoral laws were amended several times. The numerical discrepancies in his account may be due to his use of several sources. See Léon Muel, *Précis historique des assemblées parlementaires et des hautes cours de justice en France de 1789 à 1895*, Paris: 1896, pp. 59–94.

1790) against the old regime, demanding certain freedoms and rights and certain limitations on the monarchy. When this failed they resolved to behead the monarch and to establish a new form of government called a *Jumhūrīyah* (Republic). They "expelled the entire Royal family known as the Bourbon from Paris ... and the revolt (*fitnah*) continued until Napoleon assumed supreme power under the title of *Sulṭān al-Salāṭīn*."[1] When Napoleon's wars with foreign kingdoms spread, these foreign kingdoms conspired against him and succeeded ultimately in driving him out of France, despite the people's love for him. The foreign powers then brought the Bourbons back into power, enthroning Louis XVIII as the first monarch to rule France after the Revolution. This monarch, Ṭahṭāwi continued, was anxious to secure his rule by winning the approval of the French people, and so he made a "covenant between himself and the French people, by their will and with their consent, and promised to follow faithfully the terms of that law. That law was the *Sharṭah* [*la Charte*]."[2]

Ṭahṭāwi continued his account with a brief description of the vicissitudes of the reigns of Louis XVIII and of the autocratic Charles X, thus bringing his history up to the second French revolution of 1830, which he described so accurately. His description of this revolution, to which he himself was an eyewitness, is highly perceptive and articulate. He wrote:

> The French people are divided into two basic factions; the one is the monarchists, the other the libertarians [*al-Ḥurrīyah*]. By the monarchists we mean those who follow the king and assert that all affairs should be entrusted to his hands without any interference from the people. The other group is inclined toward freedom, in the sense that they claim that the law is uniquely supreme and that the king is nothing but an instrument to carry out judgments based on the laws ... Most of the followers of the king are clergymen or their disciples, while the libertarians include the philosophers and scientists, as well as most of the people. The first group attempts to aid the king while the other tries to

---

1. *Ibid.*, pp. 196–197.
2. *Ibid.* Note the fact that, although the Arabic equivalent of Constitution (*La Charte*) would be *Dustūr* and this word was actually in use at that time to mean "a body of laws," Ṭahṭāwi chose to Arabize the French term, rather than to translate it.

> weaken him and strengthen the people. Among the second group is a sizeable faction which desires to place all authority in the hands of the people, dispensing entirely with the need for a king. Since all the people cannot rule and be ruled at the same time, however, it is necessary for the people to choose from amongst themselves those who will rule. This is the rule of the republic (*Ḥukm al-jumhūrīyah*) … From this we know that some of the French advocate an absolute monarchy, others desire a limited monarchy where the king rules according to the laws, while still others want a republic.[1]

After this keen analysis of the contemporary French political scene, Ṭahṭāwi went on to explain the complex conspiracies of the monarchists to gain absolute control and the culmination of these conspiracies in the outbreak of the second French revolution. Note his grasp of basic principles in the following quotation:

> We have noted, while speaking about the laws of the French people and their rights, that Article 8 states that no Frenchman is prohibited from expressing his opinion, writing it or printing it, provided only that he does not cause any injury to what is in the laws … In the year 1830 the king issued a number of orders in which he prohibited the people from expressing, writing and printing their views … especially in the daily newspapers [*Kazīṭāt for gazettes*].[2]

The king issued these orders without consulting the National Assembly as was required by the constitution, knowing well the implications of his actions. In addition, he appointed to military positions men who were well-known for their anti-libertarian views. The revolution occurred when the people acted to prevent the resurrection of the absolute power of the king. In this revolution the people reasserted their political rights.

Ṭahṭāwi not only narrated the events which transpired during this period but, as has been indicated, also devoted considerable space

1. *Ibid.*, pp. 196–198. Contrast these fine distinctions with the confused treatment by the early Arab chroniclers of Napoleon.
2. *Ibid.*, pp. 198–199.

to an elaboration and elucidation of the French political structure. In order to explain that system more fully, Ṭahṭāwi translated the constitution of France and annotated it with detailed explanations of meaning and application. Insofar as can be determined this was the first time anything of this nature appeared in the Arabic language. This was the first time in Arab history that a document representing a coherent political system in operation in a western country was made available to an Arab-speaking audience. So alien were both the form and the content of this document that the author felt it necessary to be extremely detailed and explicit in his commentary.[1]

In the course of his translations and descriptions a number of ideas appeared which were entirely alien to the intellectual system of the Arab milieu. For example, the basic freedoms guaranteed in the French constitution were explained by Ṭahṭāwi in the following manner:

> The French people are equal before the law despite their differences in prestige, position, honor, and wealth. These latter distinctions may have utility in social convention and society, but they have no significance in the *Sharī'ah* [i.e. Constitution of France]. Therefore, all people are admitted to military and civil positions ... The *Sharī'ah* guarantees for every man the right of personal freedom so that no man can be arrested except in accordance with the terms of the laws ... And one of the corollaries of freedom among the French is that each man may pursue his own religion under the protection of the State. Whoever interferes with a man's freedom of worship is punished ... Each Frenchman has the right to express his political and religious beliefs, provided that he does not infringe on or cause damage to the order established in the statutes. All property is sacred and cannot be infringed upon; no man can be forced to give up his property unless it is required for the public interest and unless he is recompensed for its value according to a judgment handed down by the courts ... [2]

1. Significantly, the descriptions and explanations of the French political system in the work of Ṭahṭāwi and later writers show a great preoccupation with the form and structure of the system and indicate an almost total neglect of the social foundations of the system. This is not meant to minimize the importance of their work in conveying informative and suggestive material on form and structure, but it perhaps helped to set a pattern for future political thought in the Arab world, which has retained this same preoccupation to a striking degree.

2. Ṭahṭāwi, *Takhlīṣ*, p. 94; see also R. Khūri, *al-Fikr al-'Arabi al-Ḥadīth*, Beirut:

The French judicial procedure and the basis for French law were also described:

> Judges cannot be dismissed from their positions. No man can be tried except before judges in his own district. Cases are conducted publicly and criminal cases cannot be tried except in the presence of a group known as *jūrīyūn* [juries]. Punishment by confiscation of property is barred ... It would take too long to explain the legal system in effect among the French. Let us say briefly that their legal statutes are not derived from Divine Books but are taken from other laws, most of which are political. These legal statutes are therefore totally different from the *Sharī'ah* ... They are known as "French Rights," that is, the rights of Frenchmen *vis-à-vis* other Frenchmen ... [1]

That the concept of justice was recognized by Ṭahṭāwi as the most important element in the French system is indicated by this introductory remark. He noted that:

> In it [the Constitution] there are matters which those who possess reason cannot deny are a part of Justice. The meaning of *Sharṭah* (*la Charte*) in the Latin language is a piece of paper. This meaning they interpreted liberally and its name was given to the document in which the governing laws are recorded. Let us tell you about it, even though most of what is in it is not to be found in the Book of God nor in the Tradition of the Prophet (Peace Be Unto Him), so that you will understand how their reason led them to recognize that Justice and Equity are prerequisites for the welfare and well-being of states and peoples; and how the rulers and the ruled followed these laws, which permitted their countries to prosper, their knowledge to increase, their domains to expand and their hearts to be at rest. You never hear anyone complaining of injustice; Justice is the foundation of civilization.[2]

This comment was supported by Arab proverbs and sayings to emphasize the principle of justice in terms familiar to his readers.

1943, pp. 81–88.

1. Ṭahṭāwi, *Takhlīṣ*, pp. 95–96.

2. *Ibid.*, pp. 81–82. See also H. Nuseibeh, *The Ideas of Arab Nationalism*, Ithaca: 1956, pp. 108–110, 116–118.

This same emphasis on justice appeared in every other conceivable context. Thus, Article I of the Constitution met with Ṭahṭāwi's approbation:

> "That all Frenchmen are equal before the law means that the law is applied equally to them, regardless of their position and status. Even the King can be sued as everyone else and the judgment would be carried out as in any other case. See how this first principle has a great effect on the establishment of justice and in giving aid to the oppressed ... This principle is almost a unifying term for all Frenchmen, and it is one of the clearest evidences that justice has reached a high degree of perfection and that they have progressed far in the ways of civilized society."[1]

In this same manner the author elaborated on all the articles of the Constitution, revealing the essential meaning of the political principles embodied in that document. The clauses which seem to have made the deepest impression on him were those dealing with personal and religious freedoms, "even for foreigners." In addition, he acknowledged the value of the system of taxation and suggested that its adoption in Muslim lands would be most beneficial. Throughout his entire account he seems defensively aware that his readers might respond with hostility to the French principles he was enunciating, and thus he tried wherever possible to find a parallel in Arabic poetry which would at least appear similar to the more alien French concept. It is obvious from his text that he was well aware also of the complete novelty of what he was transmitting to his Arab audience, which explains his reliance on lengthy and detailed exposition.

The Arab world was indebted to Ṭahṭāwi not only for his informative accounts of the French Revolution and for his translation and anaĭysis of the French constitution, but also for his exploratory statements about the intellectual heritage of the West which had found its political expression in the liberal movements of the nineteenth century. Thus another novel aspect of his book is that it introduced Arab readers to a number of western social philosophers whose names

1. Ṭahṭāwi, *Takhlīṣ*, pp. 89–91.

had previously been unknown. In describing his liberal education in France, for example, Ṭahṭāwi informed his readers that he

> ... read a number of literary works, among which were ... sections of an anthology by Voltaire, an anthology by Rousseau containing especially his *Persian letters [sic]* in which he differentiates between Eastern and Western literature ... I also read 'Natural Law' upon which the Franks base their political order ... I also read ... a two volume work called *The Spirit of Laws* whose author is very famous among the Franks and who is called Montesquieu ... This man is referred to as the Ibn Khaldūn of the Franks just as Ibn Khaldūn might be called the Montesquieu of the Muslims ... Similarly I read a book called *The Social Contract* whose author is Rousseau. It is great in its meaning ... [1]

There can be little doubt that Ṭahṭāwi's readings in western social thought affected his attitudes. This is revealed most clearly in his independent writings on political questions and on the rights of man. There is, in his thinking on these subjects, a complete departure from the Islamic tradition which can be attributed only to the influence of the French sources he had read. Fransīs Marrāsh shared Ṭahṭāwi's admiration for the political system of France, which, in his eyes, assured continued progress for the French people and bestowed upon the nation its greatness. He noted:

> "How gratified and astonished are the eyes when they set sight on this French Nation (*al-Ummah al-Faransāwīyah*) and behold that all its components interact as if they were one piece, without conflicts among the parts nor divisions within the whole. How pleased are the eyes when they behold this nation swimming in an ocean of security and peace, fearing neither external aggression nor internal betrayal. How delighted are the eyes to see a nation enjoying its wealth without fear of a greedy beast or a covetous neighbor ... walking proudly in the wake of full liberty ... slumbering comfortably in the bed of God-given life fearing neither the sword of the blood-thirsty nor the outbreak of revolt; free to

1. *Ibid.*, pp. 185–191. It is difficult to interpret his reference to an anthology of Rousseau's works containing the *Persian Letters*. The latter were, of course, written by Montesquieu. Further, it may be that the Rousseau cited in this first part of the quotation was not the social philosopher Jean-Jacques Rousseau but rather the poet Jean-Baptiste Rousseau (1671–1741).

> exercise the Spiritual and the Mundane without fear of vilification ... or the imposition of an unjust Law ... Thus, how attracted a person is to this country that offers legitimately-gained wealth, unblemished security and unrestricted freedom ...[1]

Marrāsh recognized that the French political system was based upon two essential principles which he analyzed in the following manner:

> 1. Equality: This is one of the strongest pillars of a sound policy and the foundation of rights. It is achieved by applying the laws equally to all people, without making any distinctions among them. Thus, the strong are not aided nor are the weak oppressed ... All the people are treated equally so that the system of rights is not infringed upon.
> 2. The Public Interest: This is the most important *raison d'être* of public policy whose chief end is to safeguard this public interest ... Even if a political system were perfect ... but failed to pay attention to this principle, the society's welfare would suffer ... To uphold the public interest, five important measures are taken.
>   - A. The facilitation of education through aid to the schools, opening new schools and making it simple for people to attend such schools ...
>   - B. The facilitation of commerce through several means: shortening travel time; simplifying and making secure the means of communication; promulgating regulations to govern the conduct of business so that no one will transgress against them; and finally, eradicating all obstacles which might hinder the progress of commercial enterprises.
>   - C. The stimulation of progress in the crafts and industries by encouraging inventors through prizes, increasing the accumulation of capital [literally, material machinery] ... and increasing workshops and factories, and easing the work of the laborers.
>   - D. The assistance of agriculture by aiding the farmers and alleviating unjust treatment of this group.
>   - E. The final, which includes removing the causes of

1. Marrāsh, *Riḥlah*, pp. 34–35.

> transgressions [against rights] by protecting property, life, and dignity.[1]

Addressing himself to the same question of political organization, Khayr al-Dīn summarized the major outlines of European governments in the following terms:

> It is time now to explain the principles of their [Europeans'] political organization, principles which are the basis of their wealth and civilization which we have already described. Let it be said that the European nations, through their experience, discovered that the unlimited free reign of monarchs and statesmen in the conduct of affairs of state caused oppression and tyrannical rule which greatly injured the country … Thus they resolved to include [in the government] men who would be responsible for the conduct of public policies. Responsibility for the conduct of affairs of state was given to Ministers … They similarly resolved to institute many suitable and diversified laws. These laws are of two kinds: the first is the Public Law which governs the relationship of the government to the people; the second is the Civil Law which governs the relationships between private individuals.
>
> Contained in the former are the statements of rights and duties of the ruler and what are related to them, such as the guarantees of the people's rights and freedoms, the establishment of the forms of government – whether republic (*Jumhūrīyah*) or hereditary monarchy – the laws which are executed and the judgments of the courts, how public policy on both internal and external matters – declaring war and concluding peace and the like – is to be conducted … All these are carried out in harmony with established laws by the aid of the Ministers. These actions must meet with the approval of most of the eligible people who are the possessors of private and political rights [i.e., citizens] in France. In other countries there are often additional prerequisites to eligibility, either education or the possession of property …
>
> The second kind of laws are those used to adjudicate disputes arising out of the peoples' dealings with one another …
>
> The promulgation of laws or their amendment requires the approval of the two assemblies. These assemblies are the Upper and the Lower Houses. The Upper House is composed of the princes of the royal family and those whom the king appoints.

1. Marrāsh, *Ghābat*, pp. 46–47.

The Lower House, which is the House of Deputies (*majlis al-wukalā'*), is composed of those whom the people elect to defend their rights and oversee the activities of the government. The members of these two Houses are the responsible men of public affairs (*Ahl al-Ḥall wa al-'Aqd*) and whatever they agree upon ... becomes part of the law of the land.

The "responsibility" of Ministers means that they are directly accountable to the House of Deputies as is the case in all constitutional countries ... One of the results of such accountability is that the head of the state is dependent for the administration of his realm on the counsel of the Ministers who, in turn, cannot remain in office unless the majority of the House of Deputies is in agreement with their public policies ...

Let it also be known that the two Houses do not interfere with the details of administration, but rather, their duties are more closely connected with passing laws and watching over the government. Similarly, the two House may express opinions on any matters of internal or foreign policy presented to them by the Ministers. Also, they may question government policy and criticize it if they deem it necessary. Under such circumstances, the Ministers must answer questions and defend their policies. Such debates take place publicly, so that matters may be clear to everyone. Finally, if the majority of the House of Deputies approves the policies of the Ministers, then the latter continue in office. By such actions the public interest of the state is assuredly achieved ... If the majority of the House of Deputies, however, disapproves of the policies of the Ministers, then the King has two alternatives. First, he may replace the present Ministers; or second, he may dissolve the House of Deputies and order a new election of deputies at a specific time. If the latter is the case and if the deputies of the previous assembly are reelected, then the king may surmise that the people approved of the policies of the House of Deputies. This would indicate that a different ministry should be appointed that would be more in agreement with the policies of the majority of the assembly. If, on the contrary, the people elect deputies who favor the policies of the ministers, then the latter would continue in office ...

From the foregoing discussion it becomes apparent that the responsibilities of the two assemblies sometimes coincide and on other occasions diverge according to certain specialities peculiar to each. But the student of the principles of legislation will note that the real power resides in the House of Deputies, particularly so in the following areas: taxation, military affairs,

> accountability and responsibility of the administrative government, and the concomitant of the latter, whether the government continues in office or resigns. All these matters really depend upon the approval of the majority of the House of Deputies, even though the Upper House examines legislation to find out whether it is compatible with the principles of the constitution. Thus it is undeniable from this description that the head of state is limited by the approval of the House of Deputies which, in actual fact, represents the will of the majority of the people.
>
> It should not escape us that such restrictions are impediments to the actions of unjust princes and ministers, but Europeans have had good fortune and such success in the conduct of their worldly affairs that their monarchs and ministers perceived the great benefits which would be gained through such a system … Initially, the monarchs and ministers found these restrictions on their authority somewhat irritating and they were bitter, particularly so in view of man's natural pleasure in dominating others and in luxurious living, but the potential benefits of these restrictions revealed themselves and justified them. We are still witnessing their benefits in the progress of education, industry, agriculture, and the extraction of mineral resources from the earth. Similarly, they [the Europeans] have achieved, as a result of these restrictions, a unity between ruler and ruled to such an extent that they have been able to build up a military power impressive to other nations and sufficient to permit them to annex other territories outside of Europe … They have become a model in the way they conduct their worldly affairs which other nations have emulated and learned from. But all this could not have been accomplished without the implementation of the laws whose purpose it is to protect the liberties already described … These laws have such an important place in Europe that all the people have great respect for them and they are enforced through the continuous vigilance of the responsible men of public affairs. They are thus sufficient to protect the rights of the people, to guard their freedom and to protect the weak against the transgressions of the strong …

Drawing a moral from his observations, Khayr al-Dīn concludes his discussion with the following extremely significant statement:

> We have given sufficiently clear evidence to show the immeasurable public and private benefits which are derived from political behavior based on sound restrictive policies of government. They

> can be seen in their successful application and effects in the various [European] states. Similarly we have shown the immeasurable harm which results from uncontrolled political behavior ... *I still say that the adoption of such arrangements is imperative in our time.*[1]

The system depicted by Khayr al-Dīn was, of course, the outcome of the French Revolution, a fact which he later emphasized. It is not out of place, therefore, to examine here the comments of Khayr al-Dīn concerning the historical event which gave rise to the system so much admired by him. He noted:

> The French Revolution occurred in the year 1789 and culminated in the killing of King Louis XVI and the replacement of the monarchy by a Republic (*Jumhūrīyah*). It also gave to the French people their Constitution [transliterated directly from his Arabic; note his failure to use the Arabic equivalent] based upon human rights. This French upheaval marked a new era for human rights. This French upheaval marked a new era for human society, because it ushered the people into a new age by removing the yoke of slavery and granting them complete freedom, just as the English Revolution marked the beginning of a new era for that great nation. We must mention some of the causes of this event out of which the freedom of all Europe was born; and we must mention the conditions which prevailed in the French nation before this event and how they changed as a result of this event. Let it be known that France, before this date, had no Constitution and no orderly administration ... The land was divided into many districts (*iyālāt*) which were antagonistic to each other. The people were also divided into opposing classes ... Matters and affairs of state were not considered as a whole or in the light of the public interest but rather in terms of their bearing on personalities ... Professions and qualifications for education were highly restricted by a number of rigid rules. Religious, civil and military positions were always restricted to a certain class of people ... All the burdens of taxation and other means of support were laid upon the shoulders of the poor people, and their shoulders were weak. On the other hand, the wealthy and the members of the clergy owned about two-thirds of France and did

1. Khayr al-Dīn, *Aqwam al-Masālik fi Ma'rifat Aḥwāl al-Mamālik*, Tunis: 1867, pp. 81–89. (Italics ours.)

> not have to pay taxes to the state. All the taxes for the state had to come from the remaining third owned by the poorer classes. In addition, they had to pay taxes to the wealthy and tithes to the Church ... All in all, the people had no rights and no protections while the royal authority had no limits on it. The condition of France then was very unstable ... and she had no adequate protection against foreign invaders ... For these grievances, the French nation rose in rebellion against the state and its rulers. It replaced the old and chaotic regime with an orderly system befitting human honor and dignity. It replaced the tyranny by restrictive laws which set limits to the power of the rulers, established the equality of all persons before the law, freed industries from the old restrictions, protected the peasants from the whims of the nobility and from the tithe paid to the Church ... and unified the country. This Revolution was a symbol of freedom which opened the eyes of all nations and resulted in a number of beneficial and permanent acts.[1]

His account thus neglected almost entirely the actual course of the Revolution. Only once did he mention anything relating to it, namely the emergence of Napoleon as absolute ruler of France to put an end to the bloodshed and havoc which followed as a result of the Revolution. He condemned Napoleon's absolute rule, quoting extensively from Thiers on the undesirable course of action pursued by Napoleon. This neglect of the actual events of the Revolution does not indicate ignorance of them. Rather, his book was concerned more with the political and moral significance of the Revolution than with its operation. It may also have been true that he wished to spare his readers the frightening knowledge of the great cost at which the Revolution's advances were achieved. Thus only in passing did he indicate the political changes which transpired between 1789 and 1815. His account of these changes was brief but had no major omissions.[2]

Khayr al-Dīn's respect and admiration for the achievements of the Revolution were demonstrated in his introductory remarks on the merits of freedom, particularly in relation to the well-being and

1. *Ibid.* pp. 121–124.
2. *Ibid.*, pp. 124–132.

prosperity of the state. In his discussions of western freedom, he did not neglect other countries, but he devoted most space to France and cited her as the example. He attributed the scientific ascendency and literary and philosophical development of France to the establishment of political order based on the principles of personal and political freedom and justice which were actualized through the French Revolution. This point received considerable emphasis in his book and he supported it with familiar incidents in Islamic history and with Arabic proverbs. It is interesting to note that Khayr al-Dīn followed the same method employed by Ṭahṭāwi of citing analogies or familiar incidents to illustrate and explain essentially alien European concepts.[1]

Also similar to his predecessor, Ṭahṭāwi, Khayr al-Dīn devoted some attention to western developments in social philosophy which had furnished the intellectual basis for the Revolution. He informed his readers that Montesquieu (whom he identified as a *ḥakīm,* i.e., philosopher), in his book *Ḥikmat al-Qawānīn* (Spirit of Laws), developed the main outlines of the political system later followed in rough fashion by the French. He also mentioned that in this book the author summarized the basic rights of man and explained their meaning.

His admiration for Montesquieu, although great, was less than his idolization of Voltaire and Rousseau, who, he submitted, were the most significant men of letters and the most important architects of the system underlying the Revolution. He was somewhat distressed, however, by their attacks on religion and stated that their contributions to human welfare would have been still greater had they kept their belief in religion. Concerning Voltaire and Rousseau, he wrote: "these two great writers are the ones who inspired the French Revolution in the year 1789; they stimulated its causes and hastened its coming."[2]

Thus Khayr al-Dīn was aware both of the social and economic sources of dissatisfaction and of the development of an intellectual

1. *Ibid.*, pp. 74–77.
2. *Ibid.*, pp. 57–60.

ideology to give expression to these dissatisfactions as causes of the French Revolution. He was equally aware of the interdependence of both developments. His account of the factors which led the French people to rebel is therefore more complete and coherent than any which preceded it in the Arabic language. He was also aware of the great costs involved in the revolution and of many of the errors and transgressions committed by the revolutionists, although he believed that the ultimate results were worth the cost.

The theoretical image of the European political system as drawn by Ṭahṭāwi, Marrāsh, and Khayr al-Dīn was devoid of concrete references to mundane day-to-day operations of government. The reader of these works would have assumed that the actual operation of European governments corresponded exactly to the theoretical forms described.

One Arab writer, however, provided a complete contrast. Shidyāq paid almost no attention to theories of government but, instead, devoted large portions of his works to detailed descriptions of the daily activities of government. Through his books, the reader derived an image of actual practice against which to balance the theoretical image obtained through the works of Ṭahṭāwi, Marrāsh, and Khayr al-Dīn.

Shidyāq's discussion of the government of England, for example, dealt chiefly with administration, one of the many aspects of English culture he admired. He commended the British for:

> good administration and organization in the conduct of their affairs as well as punctuality in the performance of duties. For everything there is a special time … This quality of good administration appears clearly among their rulers, masters, and administrators. The responsible statesmen among them, if they wish to undertake an important project, approach it with meticulous care and correctness so that no fundamental changes will be necessitated in the laws and so that there will be no major disturbance to the people. For example, if they are compelled during a war to conscript men and produce boats and ammunition, all these do not necessarily cause inconvenience or confusion among the people, nor do they become the cause of a rise in the cost of living or a change in their circumstances. If the government

> wishes to impose a new tax to meet the costs of war, that matter must be taken up in the House of Commons by the representatives of the people. It is well known that a person gives more readily as a result of his representative's wishes than as a result of force by a powerful superior. In some countries, when the government decides to conscript new men into the army, one finds that people lie, exaggerate fears, the strong unjustly oppress the weak, and men take revenge on their enemies. Furthermore, the commerce of the country is upset, security among transactors ceases, and, as a result, the people within the country feel the effects of war more severely than those outside ... None of these disturbances occurred while I was in that country [England] ...
>
> One of the best effects of good administration is the sound management of the Post Office ... [A lengthy description of the British postal service followed here.][1]

While Shidyāq was favorably impressed with the efficiency of British administration, he was far less enthusiastic about how government positions were filled. He wrote: "Official appointments in England are distributed by favoritism and prejudice, never according to right or merit. If a nobleman or a man of political influence recommends one of his relatives or friends for an appointment, that recommendation is certain to be followed. Yet a person of the highest character, learning, and virtue who may be more fit for the position may fail to get an appointment because he lacks politically influential friends. Yet Englishmen in high positions do not accept bribes. If it is known that a man has taken a bribe, he is punished. And even if he offers to repay double the amount of the bribe, that cannot exonerate him."[2]

Most of Shidyāq's comments are of a similarly specific nature, although he does note in passing the role played by Parliament in formulating governmental policy. However, either he assumed that his readers were already familiar with the concept of parliamentary government or else he attached no particular significance to that institution. In any case, Shidyāq's work contains no reference to the composition of the British Parliament or to the methods whereby members of that institution were selected.

1. Shidyāq, *Kashf*, pp. 146–147.
2. *Ibid.*, p. 17.

The only other significant observation of the political system made by Shidyāq is his rather brief discussion of British law:

> British justice can be divided into four divisions. The first is what they have derived from the laws of the Romans, Normans, and Saxons, who occupied their country in the past. Among such things is Custom. As a matter of fact, most of their customs are 'Traditions' (*Sunan*) for them … The second is what is based on Justice and Equity and considerations of the public interest … The third is that which is based on laws passed by the legislature (*Majlis al-Mashūrah*) and this body of legislation is continually growing. The fourth is the general collection of rulings passed by the Council of the Church … [1]

Following this general statement, Shidyāq specifically criticized certain practices in British courts, such as the use of children as witnesses and other minor matters. Needless to say, there was no detailed statement concerning the operation of British courts. It is interesting to note, although we cannot presume to interpret its significance, that the only additional information presented on the British legal system concerned the social rank and salaries of British judges!

Private Organizations

The political organization of the European state thus captured the interest of four prominent Arab travellers. Their interest in organization, however, was not confined to the governmental level. These writers also noted the extensive cooperative organizations which Europeans had developed to serve private purposes. Some of these organizations had been developed to achieve ends which individuals working alone could never accomplish, for example, philanthropic organizations, libraries, and museums. Others, such as occupational guilds, had been developed to protect the interests of members and to pursue common economic and social goals. Still another kind – corporate associations for the pooling of capital – had provided the economic basis for European enterprises. The authors all recognized

1. *Ibid.*, p. 139.

that these non-governmental organizations had made important contributions to European progress. A point which greatly impressed some writers was the fact that these associations had been formed independent of the government, that they had grown out of the efforts of groups of individuals to meet certain economic and social needs. The novelty of this approach seemed to stimulate their interest in the functions and accomplishments of such European organizations.

Ṭahṭāwi, Shidyāq, Fransīs Marrāsh, Salīm Bustrus, and Khayr al-Dīn, as well as many of the later Arab travellers, paid careful attention to the variety of private associations which had been developed in Europe. The associations which figured most prominently in their writings were of three kinds: welfare associations, such as hospitals and other philanthropic institutions; economic associations, such as trade fairs and corporations; and cultural associations, such as libraries and museums.

Three illustrative texts on private European organizations will be discussed here. These texts represent the way in which the writers approached the subject of private organizations and the manner in which they reacted to them.

Ṭahṭāwi's description of European philanthropies is most elementary, yet it contains some searching sociological comments.

> Let it be known that most Frankish people, and indeed most people in countries where manufacture is prevalent, live by their earnings from manual work. Thus, if a person were suddenly prevented from working by an unexpected illness, for example, he would immediately lose his income and would be forced to live by other means, such as begging or the like. Thus hospital (*Māristānāt*) which serve as centers for benificence developed, so that a person would not need to beg [if he were deprived of his livelihood]. The more industrialized a country ... the more populated it is, and thus the more hospitals it needs. Since Paris is one of the most densely populated and highly industrialized places, her need for hospitals and other philanthropic institutions is very great. These ... meet the needs of the poor and compensate for the stinginess and miserliness of some of the people of Paris ... The more urbanized (*Mutaḥaḍḍirah*) a country becomes, the

> less generous her people become. They [the Frankish people] think that if they give alms to a beggar who is capable of working, they are encouraging him to be lazy. In the city of Paris there is a committee for the organization and administration of hospitals and other eleemosynary institutions. This committee has fifteen members for general consultation (*al-Mashūrah al-'āmmah*) … [Then follows a lengthy discussion of the responsibilities of each subdivision of this committee and a description of a number of philanthropic homes and hospitals.]
>
> From this it is apparent that the philanthropic activities in the city of Paris are relatively greater than in other cities … And one of the acts of charity is to collect money for someone who has been stricken suddenly so that he can begin a new life for himself … [1]

Addressing himself to the same subject, Shidyāq observed:

> Paris has thirty-six hospitals … which care for twelve thousand sick and disabled persons, both men and women. Each year more than eighty thousand persons are admitted to them. They expend about fourteen and a half million francs, although their income is even higher …
>
> Establishments [in England] are far too numerous to list. One admiring observer of London – I believe he was the famous American, Emerson – noted that the British were the most philanthropic of people. This I believe to be true without any doubt. I can briefly illustrate the more significant philanthropies which have been established by these people so that you may judge for yourselves. In London there are hospitals for the insane, for the crippled, the sick, wounded, deaf, blind, mute, needy, and for all those who have been stricken or been deprived of their means of livelihood, for those incapacitated by old age, for orphans, widows, as well as organizations for the emancipation of slaves and even the prevention of cruelty to animals. All these are in addition to their establishments for education, worship and the propagation of the Bible, which are extremely numerous … The Humane Society (*al-Jam'īyah al-Insānīyah*) performs a number of commendable services, such as the rescue of drowning people and their treatment and resuscitation … and the award of prizes to whoever saves the life of another person. Then there is also an

1. Ṭahṭāwi, *Takhlīṣ*, pp. 139–140.

> association for the aid of fire victims ... The number of hospitals and philanthropic organizations in London is over four hundred and ninety-one. [A detailed list of names and functions follows.] ... The expenditures of these establishments for all their activities exceed 1,774,733 Pounds, more than a million of which is donated by individual philanthropists ... [1]

Khayr al-Dīn viewed the proliferation of welfare institutions within the broader context of European associations, which he considered to be one of the chief foundations of the entire society. He noted that:

> From what we have shown, it should be obvious that the corporate associations (*al-Sharikāt al-*Jam'īyah) are partly responsible for the growth of commerce. The power of groups is continually apparent in various daily transactions. The more the desire for cooperation increases in a people, the more their means of living improves. For this reason, European associations have multiplied in all sorts of civic and commercial projects. Similarly, services on land and sea have increased. Learned societies and philanthropic organizations have likewise increased. The extraction of minerals, the construction of bridges, canals, railroads and the like would not have been possible without such corporations. For where is there an individual who is capable of financing such ventures by himself or who would be willing to risk his entire wealth for them? ... If the association is large and important for the public benefit, the state may guarantee a certain specified yearly profit. The administration of the association is in the hands of a group which is elected from among the stockholders and which has a greater knowledge and reputation in the law of the association ... At the end of the year, they submit an account of the activities of the company and of their administration and finally assign the dividends accordingly.
>
> Some of the greatest accomplishments of these joint corporations have been the opening of the Gulf of Suez, the construction of a railroad connecting the eastern and western parts of the United States, cutting through the Alps Mountains to connect France and Italy ... [Other important corporations include one] known as Messageries Imperiales, whose great ships are seen in every sea, and the trans-Atlantic cable, and other such facilities

1. Shidyāq, *Kashf*, pp. 300–302.

> which have emerged as a result of joint actions by statesmen, inventors and skillful professionals.
>
> ... If people join with one another to achieve a joint end, it is possible for them to attain even the most difficult things. As evidence of this, we might cite two incredible examples, the famous Bank of France and the British colonies of India. The British government, through an association of her merchants known as the India Company, acquired about three hundred million, five hundred thousand square meters of land with a population of over one hundred and eighty million persons. While the capital of the Bank of France was only thirty million Francs in 1800, representing thirty thousand shares, by 1848 it had accumulated a capital of ninety-one million Francs and had four hundred and fifty million Francs in notes among the people ... [A statement of the fluctuations of the Bank's holdings and of the services it provided follows here.] It reached this stage despite the fact that it now has many competitors, unlike its monopolistic position in the past ... [1]

These passages dealing with the political system of the European state and with the nature and extent of non-political associations indicate the emphasis Arab travellers placed on the organizational basis of European society. This ability to organize for the achievement of public and private ends was considered to be a major cause of what the travellers referred to as the "success" of European culture. While these organizations were recognized to have theoretical principles which deserved attention and explanation, in no case did the Arab travellers who wrote about them limit their discussions to abstract political and social concepts. The importance of any subject – whether constitutional government or private philanthropy – derived from its practical implications for the functioning of the social system. In many cases it is clear that the authors themselves believed that if

1. Khayr al-Dīn, *op. cit.*, pp. 77–79. Further examples of non-political organizations in the European states were also given by the authors quoted above. Trade fairs, academies, guilds, libraries, museums, and recreational facilities are also cited in the works of Ṭahṭāwi, *Takhlīṣ*, pp. 156–164; Shidyāq, *Kashf*, pp. 228–231, 275–276, 314–316; Bustrus, *al-Nazhah*, pp. 56–66, 73, 86–96; Marrāsh, *Riḥlah*, pp. 37–41, 67–72; Ḥarāyri, *'Arḍ al-Baḍā'i' al-'āmm*, Paris: 1867; and Khayr al-Dīn, *op. cit.*, pp. 69–74 and 80–81.

a similar pattern were followed in the Arab world, it would permit the Arabs to achieve similar and enviable results. Numerous allusions, sometimes explicit but more often implicit, are made to lacks and inadequacies in Arab countries which could be rectified by the adoption of certain European institutions and patterns of cooperative organization.

Three observations might be made concerning the attitudes of these Arab travellers toward European political and social organizations. First, their preoccupation with constitutional government seems to have been motivated by both a deeply sympathetic response to the concept of *limiting* the ruler's power and a belief that such limitations would in themselves stimulate economic progress in the Arab world.[1]

Second, the emphasis placed on civic responsibility in private welfare and other non-governmental organizations seems to have been motivated chiefly by their acknowledgment that the Arab world had a great need for many of the services rendered by such organizations. The *Awqāf* (philanthropies administered through the religious institutions) were deficient and Arab governments uninterested in performing many of the functions desired by the authors. In the private organizations of Europe they saw models of how many of their social needs could be met, even in the absence of governmental action.

Third, the authors stressed the organic unity of European society and the interrelationships between private associations and governmental organization. The fact that each supported the other, complemented the functions of the other, and facilitated or improved the operations of the other made a deep impression on the travellers who, in turn, transmitted this impression to their readers. Thus, it was not constitutional government alone nor was it the private welfare, economic, and cultural associations alone, but the working together of both sectors that had made European progress possible.

1. The authors seem to have been unaware of the fact that this process had actually been in the reverse order in Europe. While economic development in Europe was undoubtedly facilitated by constitutional government, economic development leading to the emergence of the bourgeoisie was also a precipitating factor in the eventual achievement of a constitutional form of government. Of this the writers took no note.

Although many features of the European political and social scene were perceived to be significant by the travellers, one of the most crucial bases of that order, namely nationalism, was either ill-understood or ignored altogether. The Arab travellers to Europe used the terms *millah* and *ummah* interchangeably and, in all cases, used them in their traditional Islamic context. As an independent and unique concept, nationalism in its later and contemporary meaning did not strike a sensitive chord. At no point in their discussions did the Arab travellers consider it necessary to communicate to their readers the meaning of the concept and its relevance to the evolution of the European state.

It is also significant to note that the Arabic term which was later used to designate nationalism, *qawmīyah*, never appears in the literature of this early period, either in the translations or in the travel accounts. What does appear is the term *waṭanīyah*, i.e. patriotism. Europeans were thought to have developed their feelings of loyalty to the *patrie* because the state adhered to the principles of constitutionalism and granted freedom to the individual. This view, that there was a reciprocal relationship between one's loyalty to his *patrie* and what that *patrie* offered him in return, was to figure significantly in later Islamic political thought, particularly in Egypt.[1]

1. Sylvia Haim's discussion, "Islam and Arab Nationalism," in Walter Laqueur, ed., *The Middle East in Transition*, New York: 1958, pp. 280–307, takes as its starting point the post-1870 writings. For an early illustration of this, see R. Riḍa, *Ta'rīkh al-Ustādh al-Imām al-Shaykh Muḥammad 'Abduh*, Vol. II, Cairo: 1926, pp. 194–195; for a contemporary view, see M. Razzāz, *Taṭawwur Ma'na al-Qawmīyah*, Beirut: 1957, translated by I. Abu-Lughod, *The Evolution of the Meaning of Nationalism*, New York: 1963, pp. 16–21.

SIX

Travellers' Views of Europe: The Educational System and the Social Order

Education and Learning

Another facet of European culture which deeply impressed the Arab travellers of the nineteenth century was the emphasis on education and learning. While some of the travellers merely noted the existence of such an emphasis with approving platitudes, others were so affected that they undertook a more or less detailed description of how the system operated and of the assumptions upon which it was based.

Since the treatment of education in the various works differs, excerpts have been selected from the works of those travellers whose accounts contained the fullest substantive comments on European education. Prior to 1870, detailed comments were to be found chiefly in the books of Ṭahṭāwi, Shidyāq, and Khayr al-Dīn. In these works, the authors explicitly noted that European progress in political, scientific, and economic affairs could not have occurred withour prior progress in the field of education.

So little was known concerning "western" forms of learning that the first author, Ṭahṭāwi, found it necessary to familiarize his readers with even the subjects included in a European education:

> The Franks have divided human knowledge into two parts, the Arts and the Sciences. Science deals with the proven phenomena of perception; art is the knowledge of the way a thing is created according to certain principles. Science is in turn subdivided into the mathematical and the non-mathematical sciences. Among the mathematical sciences are arithmetic, geometry, algebra, and

> calculus; the non-mathematical sciences include physics, theology, natural history – including botany, zoology, geology, and the like – and chemistry. Theology is sometimes called metaphysics.
>
> The Arts are also divided into two kinds. One of these is the intellectual arts, which are very close to the sciences ... [They] include rhetoric, grammar, logic, poetry, painting, drawing, sculpture, and music. All these are intellectual arts because they require scientific principles. The second group is referred to as the applied arts, which include the crafts and industries. This is the way the Frankish philosophers divide their knowledge, while in our lands we draw no such distinctions ... Arithmetic, geometry, geography, history, and drawing are required subjects for all students. All these must be taken after a mastery of the language. [A lengthy statement is included here on the French language, with emphasis on the simplification of scientific terminology for the student.][1]

The fact that the educational system was open to females as well as males elicited an enthusiastic if somewhat incredulous response from Ṭahṭāwi. Speaking on the role of European women in the intellectual life of those countries, he observed:

> European women have written profound books. Among them [educated women] are some who translate books from one language to another ... The themes and compositions of some of these women are taken as models according to which others design their works. From this, one knows that the proverb "Man's beauty is his brain, while woman's beauty is her tongue" is not a fitting description for this country.[2]

The effect of these observations on Ṭahṭāwi's later attitudes toward the education of women must have been considerable. It led him eventually to accept the legitimacy of female education in the Arab world. To implement this he later advocated the establishment of a school for girls in Egypt and, in fact, wrote the first textbook prepared specifically for use by both sexes.[3]

1. Ṭahṭāwi, *Takhlīṣ*, pp. 221–222. See also the much briefer statement of Marrāsh, *Riḥlah*, p. 37.
2. Ṭahṭāwi, *Takhlīṣ*, p. 76.
3. The textbook, in which Ṭahṭāwi also defended his "novel" ideas concerning the

Ṭahṭāwi also felt a deep admiration for the vitality of French education and pursuit of new knowledge and for the scholars who devoted themselves to these ends. Thus he wrote of them:

> Their scholars (*'Ulamā'*) ... are well-versed in a number of fields and are specialists as well in one subject. They explore many areas and make many new discoveries ... These are the qualities which distinguish the scholar. Not every teacher or author is a scholar, and do not imagine that the French scholars are the priests. The latter are scholars only in the religious field, although it is possible for a priest to become a scholar [if he possesses the qualities noted above]. In other words, scholarship is an attribute of the person who has a great deal of knowledge in the intellectual sciences ... The virtue of these Christians in the attainment of learning is readily apparent. It is also apparent that our own country is devoid of such achievements. The Azhar, the Umayyad ... and the rest of the Muslim schools are distinguished by their emphasis on traditional learning (*Naqlīyah*) and on certain intellectual fields such as logic and Arabic literature ... But scientific progress in Paris is continually developing. No year passes without the addition of some new discovery. They [the French] might even add in the space of one year a number of new arts, industries, methods or techniques ...[1]

It is obvious from Ṭahṭāwi's account that he perceived the essential differences between Near Eastern and western scholarship. The essence of the latter was the concept that neither knowledge nor the process of education was finite. This concept was one with which Ṭahṭāwi definitely concurred and he described with open praise the European approach to the scholarly life. He informed his readers, for example, that the European scholar did not cease his education after completing his formal training but viewed the latter as merely the first step in the attainment of knowledge. He also emphasized that the mission of the European scholar was not to master what was already known so that he could transmit that knowledge intact to

---

importance of female education, was entitled *al-Murshid al-Amīn Lilbanāt wa al-Banīn* (The Honest Guide for Girls and Boys), Cairo: 1872. See particularly pp. 4, 40–41, and 60.

1. Ṭahṭāwi, *Takhlīṣ*, p. 155.

his students but rather to use that knowledge as a point of departure, adding to it and modifying it according to the fruits of his own investigations. To this spirit of continuous inquiry he attributed Europe's capacity to enrich herself through the pursuit of knowledge.[1]

Ṭahṭāwi's chief interest was in the educational system at the university level, and he therefore included little material on the primary and secondary levels of education. His description of the higher level of education, however, was detailed and specific. For example, he wrote:

> In Paris there are five governmental schools (*Madāris Sulṭānīyah*) which are called *Collèges* [pronunciation given]. These are the schools in which one learns the important sciences … In these five schools, composition and writing, ancient foreign languages, principles of physics, … drawing and calligraphy are taught. The students are graded into different stages. Each year the student graduates to the next stage. The years of instruction are six, and the student is promoted to the next year upon the completion of the preceding year … There are two more colleges which are non-governmental (*Ghayr Sulṭānīyah*) and which teach all the subjects given in the other five. Then there is another college called the College of the French, which is the greatest of them all. In it one can learn mathematics, physics mixed with mathematics [presumably pure physics], applied physics, geography, medicine … , languages such as Arabic, Persian, Turkish, Hebrew, Syriac, Chinese … , Greek philosophy, rhetoric, Latin, and French language and literature. This college includes the greatest scholars and has six thousand students. One of its most famous schools is the *Polytechnique* [pronunciation given] in which mathematics and physics are taught for the training of engineers in geography and military affairs. The geography engineers [civil engineers] design bridges, roads and sidewalks, canals and the like. The military engineers design fortifications, towers, and plants for the manufacture of munitions … The responsible personnel of this school are real researchers who have an extensive knowledge in various sciences. It is a complete honor for a person to be a student in this school …[2]

1. *Ibid.*, pp. 60, 154.
2. *Ibid.*, pp. 165 ff.

Following this description of the French colleges, Ṭahṭāwi presents similar information concerning technical institutes and schools for non-scientific studies, such as law schools and schools of fine arts. His chief concern was with the variety of subjects taught in western schools, rather than with the administrative organization of the educational system.

The breadth and depth of the French approach to learning were the aspects of education which he most admired. These he regarded as the outgrowth of two basic factors. In the first place, the Europeans apparently had a natural inclination toward learning and a spontaneous sense of curiosity and inquiry. This, Ṭahṭāwi believed, was an important element in the development of their intellectual life. Second, he recognized the fundamental role played by the government in encouraging free inquiry and in offering facilities conducive to scholarly pursuits. The government, by acknowledging education as a fundamental *right* of all people, regardless of class, contributed ideologically to the development of education. In addition, the government made concrete contributions by aiding such educational adjuncts as libraries and scholarly journals and, even more important, by giving direct assistance to scholars. Among the governmental aids to scholars he listed prizes to those who had made substantial contributions to learning, and protection of the rights of scholars by publicizing their works in newspapers and copyrighting their material. For all of these things Ṭahṭāwi had nothing but admiration.

Ṭahṭāwi, by describing the western approach to learning and western institutions for the dissemination of knowledge, made a basic contribution to the entire process of transmitting western ideology to the Arab world. His was the first source of information about the content and context of modern European scholarship. In his book was the first suggestion that Europe's technical achievements had not developed in a vacuum but were rather the by-products of an entire *Weltanschauung* in which free inquiry and unfettered scholarship were accepted and even encouraged. Later writings on the same subject were to draw heavily on his analysis.[1]

1. See, for example, Shidyāq, *Kashf*, pp. 225–227; Khayr al-Dīn, *Aqwam al-Masālik*

In comparison with Ṭahṭāwi's comprehensive and analytical treatment of the French educational system, Shidyāq's account seems superficial on the theoretical level. Nevertheless it adds a dimension of concreteness to supplement the former's more cosmic approach. Shidyāq, contrasting the British and French systems of education, for example, observed that

> it is easier to acquire knowledge and crafts in France than in Britain ... because schools [in France] are more numerous and less expensive as well as better organized, so much so that Britons send their children to Paris to study there what is more difficult to learn in England ... [1]

The only other observation on education made by Shidyāq is one concerning higher education in England.

> Cambridge and Oxford are two English cities, each containing about twenty schools and two thousand students. In the former, geometry, mathematics, and theology are taught, while in the latter, literature, law, logic, and philosophy are the subjects of instruction ... It is impossible to obtain an education there without incurring very heavy expenses and no one goes there except students who are very rich and from the upper class. This is particularly true at Oxford, where students are very boastful, as if they were seeking the kingdoms of India and China. Most of the students spend their time in horseback riding and other pleasures ... When the day of examination approaches, the student then tries to find out which things the professor is going to examine him on and does his best to study those things very well. If the student manages to do well in these subjects, then his professor licenses him, indicating that the student is prepared to teach others ...
>
> For each of the schools there are endowments (*Awqāf*) from which the resident priests and non-priests, who are called Fellows, derive their incomes ... He who has excelled in his field can obtain a livelihood from these endowments ... provided he remains unmarried ... At a certain day each year there occurs a brawl between the people of the town and the students ... which

fi Ma'rifat Aḥwāl al-Mamālik, Tunis: 1867, p. 69.

1. Shidyāq, *Kashf*, pp. 273–274.

> is called the day of the Gown and the Town, because the students wear gowns ... In each of these towns there is an Arabic library, although the Oxford library is better and contains more books. All the books in this library, Arabic as well as others, total about three hundred thousand ...[1]

Shidyāq also remarked unfavorably concerning British orientalists, impugning their knowledge of Arabic among other things. However, his account did bring out the fact that Arabic was being taught in England and that Arabic books were part of the library collections in several schools. Like Ṭahṭāwi, he was impressed by the extensive libraries of Europe and by their efficient and simple organizational techniques.[2]

Fransīs Marrāsh took cognizance of the extent to which the government supported education, which he greatly approved. He was interested in the fact that the state bestowed monetary and honorific awards on scholars who made important contributions in their special fields. And he stressed that European progress was inextricably related to educational advances on all levels. However, he did not attempt to describe the educational system itself.[3]

This task remained for Khayr al-Dīn, who wrote, insofar as can be ascertained, the first comprehensive analysis of the French educational system to appear in Arabic, and, indeed, the first comprehensive discussion of *any* educational system in modern Arabic literature. His discussion of education in France was prefaced by a lengthy chronicle of European discoveries since the fifteenth century, all of which he considered the outgrowth of intellectual advances. He wrote:

1. *Ibid.*, p. 127. It is interesting to contrast the glowing description of French dedication to the pursuit of knowledge given by Ṭahṭāwi with the image of proud, pleasure-loving, end-of-term cramming English students described by Shidyāq. We may assume that the contrast derives at least in part from the predispositions of the Arab observers, although undoubtedly there were real differences between French and English society of the time. Again, Ṭahṭāwi was concerned with the ideal of scholarship held by the West whereas Shidyāq, the social observer, was concerned more with the actual manifestations.
2. *Ibid.*, pp. 314–317.
3. Fransīs Marrāsh, *Riḥlah*, pp. 40–42. The statements of Bustrus are more indirect. See his *al-Nuzhah*, pp. 18–27, 35, 54, 73.

Since the progress of European civilization, from which resulted the aforementioned discoveries, was possible only through the evolution of learning in Europe, and since the French state has acquired fame for its orderly educational administration, we have seen fit to portray its successful organization at the various educational levels. The remainder of the European States have followed the French pattern closely; thus, the reader should be able to understand them on the basis of his knowledge of the French system.

Let it be known that education is in three stages, Elementary, Intermediate, and Advanced. Accordingly, learning is divided into these three stages with regards to its complexity or simplicity.

The elementary stage includes instruction in ethics, principles of theology, reading, writing, language, elementary mathematics, weights and measures, history and geography, physics, geology, agriculture, crafts, hygiene … and physical education. These elementary skills are taught in schools set up by the national and local governments, in addition to private schools …

The intermediate stage, which is commenced after the completion of the first stage, includes instruction in ancient and modern languages and in philosophy, mathematics, physics and history. All these arts and sciences are taught in the aforementioned schools.

The final stage is for those who attend universities or who attend classes held by certain professors who have the right to license qualified students. The universities teach theology, law (*Aḥkām al-Nawāzil*), rhetoric and the like. The universities are of five types:

1. One type includes eight colleges whose function is to teach theology. Six of these colleges teach theology according to the Catholic Faith, while the remaining two teach theology according to the Protestant Faith … The obligations of the faith, ethics, the system of the Church, the Book, which is described as Holy by them, and the Hebrew language are among the branches of this science.
2. The second type of university includes nine colleges whose function is the teaching of ʿIlm al-Nawāzil, which includes general principles of conduct, Roman Law, Civil Law, Criminal Law, Jurisprudence, Commercial Law, Public Administration and International Law …
3. The third type includes three colleges whose function is

to teach medicine, zoology, natural history, principles of obstetrics ... There are also special schools for pharmacy.

4. The fourth type includes colleges whose function is to teach other sciences, such as geography, astronomy, algebra, archeology, chemistry, geology, botany, and the like.
5. The fifth type includes colleges which teach literature and related subjects, philosophy and the history of philosophy, ancient and modern history ...

> Finally, there are special schools not included above, such as the School of France [possibly the *Collège de France*], the School of Oriental Languages, ... the School of Fine Arts, the School of Dramatics, and the like. All the schools and universities discussed are under the supervision of the Minister of Education and, while the private schools are not under his direction, they conform closely to the system prevailing in the governmental schools and are occasionally inspected by the Ministry ...[1]

This, essentially, was the outline of the French educational system which Khayr al-Dīn transmitted to the Arabic reading public. Despite its many omissions and inadequacies, it did permit the reader to grasp clearly the differences, in terms of both organization and content, between the prevailing Near Eastern system and the system in Europe. It introduced the reader to subjects which he may not have known and to the idea that Europeans were interested in the language and culture of the Arabs as well as other foreign countries. While it is impossible to trace directly the eventual impact of such information, one may assume that Khayr al-Dīn's account of European education was not entirely ineffectual in shaping future educational policies in the Arab world.

In short, all five Arab travellers writing prior to 1870 noted, with varying degrees of detail and emphasis, the nature and value of the educational system prevailing in Europe. They noted also the role of the state in fostering the educational training of its citizens and the complementary role of learned societies, such as the *Académie Française*, in promoting critical interest in learning and the exchange of scientific and cultural information. In general, their impressions of

---

1. Khayr al-Dīn, *op. cit.*, pp. 65–69.

European learning and education were extremely favorable, and they advocated the adoption of similar patterns in their own countries. Only Shidyāq expressed any criticism of western education, and his criticisms were directed to the abuses of the system rather than to the system itself.

Miscellaneous Sociological Observations

The subjects discussed above were dealt with by several travellers, each adding to the material of the other. However, there were many other aspects of European life which captured their individual interests but concerning which no general conclusions or "trends" can be established. Among the subjects given special attention by individual writers were three particularly significant aspects of European culture: the role of the western woman; the class structure of European society; and the position of religion in European life and politics. The early comments on these questions by Arab travellers have become incorporated into Arab culture and have served to foster stereotypes of Europeans which are still commonly held throughout the Arab world.

ROLE OF WESTERN WOMAN

Ṭahṭāwi recognized the prominent position occupied by women in French society. In addition to participating in the intellectual life of the country,[1] the French woman also took part in the daily transactions of business. Thus, Ṭahṭāwi points out, "it is the custom in this country to assign the activities of buying and selling to the women, while the men perform other tasks."[2] His image of the French woman was, however, not an altogether complimentary one. For example, he stated that "Paris can be described as the Paradise of Women but the Hell of Men"[3] – a fact which he attributed to the independence of women and their "different" social status. In addition he criticized what he described as

1. See above, p. 116.
2. Ṭahṭāwi, *Takhlīṣ*, p. 40.
3. *Ibid.*, p. 67.

> ... the lack of moral purity among a great number of French women. Their men are not jealous ... What can one expect in this country where adultery is considered a vice or a shame, rather than a sin? Men in these lands are slaves to women ... Their women's transgressions are many ... It is well known that purity of the women exists only in the middle class, but not in the upper or lower classes ...[1]

Ṭahṭāwi, however, rejected the idea that the lack of moral purity on the part of French women resulted merely from their failure to veil. He noted: "The questionable virtues of French women should not be blamed on their failure to veil but rather on the true causes, which are to be found in the nature of their training, in their devotion (or lack thereof) to a single person, and on an incompatibility between husbands and wives ... "[2] Ṭahṭāwi's other observations about French women concerned chiefly their frivolous clothes and their excessive preoccupation with appearance.[3]

While Shidyāq also mentioned women in his book, his comments add nothing to the picture already drawn by Ṭahṭāwi. He dealt chiefly with the physical appearance of European women and was somewhat more detailed and less complimentary than Ṭahṭāwi.[4]

CLASS STRUCTURE

Only Shidyāq seems to have been interested in the social structure of European society. In his work alone one finds reference to the system of social stratification which characterized European life at that time. Shidyāq's discussion was motivated by his desire to describe the customs of the English people and by his recognition that these customs varied from class to class. His analysis of the English class structure and his comparisons between French and English cultures are presented below:

---

1. *Ibid.*, pp. 251–252.
2. *Ibid.*, p. 251.
3. *Ibid.*, pp. 105–108, 112–113.
4. For illustrations, see Shidyāq, *al-Sāq*, pp. 635–644; and *Kashf*, pp. 158–159, 254–255, 256–257.

> These people [the English] can be divided into five classes. The first class includes the princes, ministers [Cabinet Ministers], the nobility, others in very high positions, and the Bishops. The second class includes the notables [*A'yān*] who live on income derived from their properties rather from their professions; they do not possess high title. The third class includes scholars, jurists, lawyers, priests, and industrialists [important businessmen]. The fourth class includes small businessmen, professional writers … In the fifth class are to be found the craftsmen and laborers, followed by the peasants. These constitute the greatest majority of the people.[1]

These classes share many customs, but there are other customs which are unique to particular classes.

> The mores and customs of the first class are somewhat similar to those of the second, while between these two and the fifth class there is practically nothing in common … The third and fourth classes resemble each other … All the classes have certain qualities in common, namely, a love of the fatherland, pride in what they possess, respect and obedience for the laws upon which the whole fabric of their society rests. Since the last class constitutes the greatest majority and since they constitute the real Britons, having remained true to their ancient customs and mores and having not mixed with other peoples either directly or through reading, it is necessary to discuss them first. The first quality which distinguishes these people is their lack of interest in strangers … nay, they do not even bother about their neighbors … Every one of these people is concerned only with his own work and scarcely desires to know anything about any other matter … It is possible to say that the real reason for the greatness and strength of the British country is that the people (*al-Ra'īyah*) do not bother to oppose the responsible men nor do they pry into what their masters or their representatives see fit to do. For this reason an uprising or revolution is not likely to occur, unlike the case in France, where everyone takes an interest in the affairs of the responsible men … These people are so obedient to their masters that even if the latter ordered them to cease cohabiting with their wives, the people would comply …
>
> Another characteristic of these people is their dullness and

1. *Ibid.*, pp. 112–113.

slowness [of mind]. Their children can hardly understand a stranger and even their elders cannot understand what they are told until they have thought it over very carefully. Oh, what a difference between them and the French, whose children answer a question with such alacrity that one feels they have studied it even before the question was asked! … Also they show no respect for the aged nor do their children fear their elders as our children do. Their fathers have little kindness for their children and thus it often happens that fathers kill their own sons. It is also possible for a father to commit incest with his own daughter, which is, however, even more common among the French. But I have not heard that a son may do the same with his mother. However, it is possible for the mother to join with the daughter in committing corrupt and vile acts … I have criticized these customs and habits of the English people because these things contrast with their great achievements in the arts and sciences which should have purified their character … What I have criticized in them has been agreed to by some of them who have travelled in the East and acquired some of our customs. All of them admit that these characteristics of the common people of Britain during this age, which is the age of refinement, are quite despicable.

I will conclude my remarks by saying that the common class of Britain is quite inferior to that of France in manners and refinement, although the British upper classes are superior to the upper classes in France. I will also say that, despite what has been said incorrectly that the Frankish states aspire to educate their people, this is not true. It is not in the interest of either the state or the church to have an educated and knowledgeable commonalty; especially in the case of the French, education of the commonalty has resulted in criticism of the government and has been responsible for the fact that more changes have taken place in France than in any other country … [1]

The men are not harsh in their treatment of women. Thus, if a man came home to find another man speaking with his wife, he would not immediately engage in name-calling but would first ascertain the cause of the other man's presence … Also, they encourage their children to work and acquire economic independence. They train their children to be patient and persevering, no matter whether the task is important or not. They do not cease trying and they do not find comfort in laziness. None of

1. *Ibid.*, pp. 112–145.

> them will say "I am too old to learn." … Most of their activities in youth are devoted to preparing for old age.
>
> Then, although the love of one's country is implanted in everyone's nature and it is natural for one to prefer his own country, yet … this quality seems to be particularly evident in British character. Whenever they travel, they continue to speak of their own country and always mention how they prefer it … I have seen many who travelled in our country … and others who spoke highly of other places … but in the end they would say, "there is nothing like Good Old England." Old England is described as such because it has remained unchanged in its customs and conditions … One finds the English travelling in all countries and crossing all seas; yet one never finds one among them who travels to learn painting, dancing, or singing as is true of other Frankish people. All their travel is for commercial purposes, while the rich and nobles travel for recreation or to decrease their heavy expenses at home … [1]

Shidyāq described many other aspects of British society, but little purpose would be served by quoting at greater length from his book. Suffice it to say that much of the book is devoted to similar observations, which rely either on the author's own observations, on hearsay, or, in some cases, on newspaper accounts. (This latter was undoubtedly the source of his impression that "fathers killing sons" was a common occurrence in England!) It is perhaps significant, however, that none of the other travellers addressed himself to similar questions.

POSITION OF RELIGION IN EUROPEAN LIFE

Several writers mentioned the religious aspects of European life, although few devoted much attention to this topic. Ṭahṭāwi did include a brief discussion of the religious affiliation of the French and of the relationship between religion and the state. He wrote:

> We have mentioned that, according to the Charter, the official religion of the state is Christianity according to the Catholic Rite. This provision was stricken after the last revolution [1830].

---

1. *Ibid.*, pp. 152–153.

> However, they acknowledge the Pope, who is the King of Rome, to be the primate of all Christians and the leader of their faith. Just as Catholicism is the official religion of the state, so also is it the religion of the majority of the people. There exists in Paris a Christian group known as Protestants as well as other Christian groups, and there are many Jews who have found residence there, but there are no Muslims who have come to live there. We have also mentioned that the French are Christians in name only and do not pay attention to the prohibitions and obligations of the religion … The priests are not exalted in this country, except within their Churches … as if they were the enemies of enlightenment and knowledge. It is said that the majority of the Frankish kingdoms are like the city of Paris … [A critical statement inserted by de Sacy to the effect that Ṭahṭāwi's observations do not apply to other parts of the country was dismissed by Ṭahṭāwi on the grounds that de Sacy was a priest and therefore biased.] One of the ordinary but deplorable customs in France and all Catholic countries is celibacy of priests, no matter what their rank. Their inability to marry increases their corruption and little else. One of the despicable customs is that priests insist that the people confess all their sins to them to gain forgiveness … It is known among them that most of the people going to confession are women and children … [The remainder of Ṭahṭāwi's account concerns the ranks of the Catholic clergy.][1]

A somewhat different view appears in Shidyāq's description of the religious affiliations of the British. In his usual disillusioning manner he noted:

> … Most of the peasants attend church out of social pressure from their neighbors or from fear of the priests who have extensive power over the people. When the prayers are held, these peasants yawn or feign sleepiness … Let it be known that the Established Church is headed by two archbishops, the Archbishop of Canterbury, whose yearly income is twenty-five thousand pounds, and the Archbishop of York, whose yearly income is fifteen thousand pounds. Next in rank come twenty-five thousand priests, each of whom receives four or more thousand pounds yearly … [The numbers and salaries of all lower priests are given.] The total revenue of the Church of England amounted to 466,311

1. Ṭahṭāwi, *Takhlīṣ*, pp. 148–151.

> pounds in the year 1854 … The Established Church has the right to collect tithes from the rest of the churches; even the Jews pay it … It is possible to say that the Established Church is one of the *Dīwāns* of the state. The title Rector of the village is much more important than the title Officer of the village … It is more suitable to call him the Chief of the town … One finds that he has the best house, servants, carriages with a private driver … and when he ascends the pulpit to preach, he advises the poor people to be ascetic and avoid the temptations of life! … It is absolutely necessary that an established church should exist in every village, even though that village may lack a shop to sell the necessities of life … Voltaire said that the English lands are the lands of sects and rituals. While the Englishman may go to heaven in any way he wishes and while he may worship God in any way he pleases, nevertheless, the only means of gaining wealth or achieving a high position in the state is by belonging to the Established Church. It is impossible for a person in England or Ireland to acquire an office if he does not belong to the Anglican Church (*al-Kanīsah al-Usqufīyah*). This condition has made all the important persons in the state members of the party of the Church. And the clergy of this Church have adopted all the customs of the Catholic Church, especially in the collection of tithes, in greed and in power over the people. The rector of the village is nothing but a would-be Pope, although most of them are more circumspect than the French clergy … [Shidyāq corrects this last statement by stating that "French priests nowadays are models of virtue and good works."][1]

Indicating the power of the clergy in England, Shidyāq drew an analogy between the position of high priests and of government Cabinet ministers. Thus, he wrote:

> The priests have almost the same rank as Cabinet ministers. For example, the First Lord of the Admiralty has an income of about forty-five thousand pounds. In the same way those "God-fearing" priests resemble Cabinet ministers in their accumulation of wealth and power, they also resemble them in exaltation of their influence and their aloofness from the ordinary citizen. An interview with the Archbishop is, for example, more difficult to obtain than one with Prince Albert, the husband of the present queen …

1. Shidyāq, *Kashf*, pp. 183–197.

> The English ascribe pomposity and extravagance to the Eastern Churches ... while the truth of the matter is that these are the very characteristics of the English Church. It is easier to meet the Archbishop of Antioch than to meet a British Archbishop.[1]

Of French religion he had less to say. Aside from a factual description of the religious affiliation of the French, he made no comments on the position of the Catholic Church in the power structure of French society. His reference to religion in France was confined to the following:

> The population of France is 32,500,000, of which two and a third millions are Protestants and Jews ... In the year 1843, there were about twenty-four thousand priests, of whom three were cardinals, fourteen were archbishops, and sixty-seven were bishops ... The number of the clergy at the time of the Revolution was 114,000, of whom 32,000 were nuns ... Total expenditures for Catholicism annually are 34,251,000 francs; for Protestantism, 1,033,000 francs; and for Judaism, 90,000 francs ...[2]

In addition to this statement, Shidyāq comments in passing concerning the fact that the French people were really no more irreligious than the English but were merely franker about showing their disinterest in religion.

These impressions of religion in the West ignored large areas of religious observance in Europe. Despite their paucity, however, they constituted the core of Arab comprehension of the role of religion and the relationship between religion and the state in Europe prior to 1870. While it is difficult to draw convincing conclusions from such uneven accounts, it does seem that an Arab reader deriving his image from these sources would have remained totally unaware of the secular nature of the European state and of the rigid ideological separation between Church and state envisaged by later Arab nationalists, for the travellers themselves seem to have been unaware of secularism as a concept or of its implications for political life.

1. *Ibid.*, pp. 322–323.
2. *Ibid.*, pp. 222–223.

In addition to the above quotations, the only other contexts in which religion was even mentioned concerned the general rebellion against the clergy and the confiscation of their properties during the French Revolution, and the guarantee of freedom of worship contained in the French Constitution.[1] This latter can scarcely be interpreted to mean "secularism," since the concept of religious tolerance was neither foreign to Muslims nor related in their minds to secularism in the modern sense. Rather than giving an impression of secularism, these books created the undeniable impression that Catholicism still received the support and protection of the French state while the Anglican Church occupied a similarly exalted position in England.[2]

1. See Ṭahṭāwi as quoted on page 93

2. It has been suggested by Bernard Lewis that one of the most important elements which made the French Revolution and post-revolutionary France attractive to Muslims was its secular nature. According to his view, the secularism of the Revolution freed France and her achievements from an association with Christianity, thus making it possible for Muslims, for the first time, to examine the West objectively. This argument is developed in his article, "The Impact of the French Revolution on Turkey: Some Notes on the Transmission of Ideas," *Journal of World History*, Paris: 1953, Vol. 1, No. 1, pp. 105–115, and reiterated in his subsequent book *The Emergence*, p. 54. Our investigation of the chief sources of Arab-Muslim reaction to post-revolutionary France fails to substantiate his view. Quite to the contrary, the Muslim Arabs whose works have been analyzed here continued to view France as a Christian country. Their criticisms, interestingly enough, were directed against this very lack of religious ardor, with one writer specifically disturbed by the absence of religious fervor and another upset by the anti-religious bias of the Revolution. Professor Lewis' hypothesis seems to have been based chiefly on a few official Ottoman sources. However, its application even to Turkish Islam has been seriously questioned by a Turkish investigator who, using the same and additional sources, concluded that "the 'secularism' of which he [Lewis] speaks ... never affected the staunchly conservative masses." See Şerif Mardin, *The Genesis of Young Ottoman Thought: A Study in the Modernization of Turkish Political Ideas*, Princeton: 1962, pp. 169–170.

SEVEN

Arab Attitudes and Reactions to Western Achievements

By 1870, as we have seen, Arab intellectuals had acquired a fairly extensive if not always balanced knowledge of the major political, social, economic, and educational developments of western culture. This knowledge came in large part either from original French works rendered into Arabic by native translators or through first-hand impressions of Europe as recorded by Arab travellers to the West. By that time, such knowledge had begun to affect the intellectual climate, especially that of the younger generation of educated Arabs. This group in turn began to exert pressure on the older, more traditionally educated intellectual leaders to alter their society in conformity with the western model.

Three events, all occurring in the 1870s, are symptomatic and indicative of the shifts which were then taking place. First, a noted Lebanese writer felt impelled to caution the youth of his day against the indiscriminate imitation of western habits and customs – what he termed excessive *tafarnuj* (literally, frankification). This writer, Buṭrus al-Bustāni, was well acquainted with western culture and, in fact, was an admirer of many aspects of that culture, so that his admonition cannot be dismissed as bigoted isolationism. In his work the writer compared the evolution of European and Arab customs for the avowed purpose of demonstrating that one was not necessarily nor inherently superior to the other.[1] The theme of his book is understandable only in the context of the frankophilic attitudes widely held by the educated youths of Lebanon.

1. B. al-Bustāni, *Khiṭāb fi al-Hay'ah al-Ijtimā'īyah*, Beirut: 1869, pp. 3–6.

Second, Ḥasan al-Marṣifi, an Egyptian Muslim of the traditionally educated older generation, wrote a book concerned solely with the new subjects discussed by the younger intellectuals. In this book he attempted to interpret these political concepts to make them more compatible with the traditionalist views. He dealt with the "new" concepts, such as nation, patriotism, the state, etc. – subjects which, prior to the influx of information about the West, would not have been considered appropriate to a learned book. That a traditional scholar addressed himself to such matters is in itself a sensitive index to how much of a revolution had occurred in the intellectual climate of the Arab world.[1]

A third indication of the great changes which were occurring as a result of the influence of western ideas was the movement to reorganize al-Azhar University. For centuries, al-Azhar had been the cornerstone of conservatism and immutability in the Arab world. That pressure to change its orientation and curriculum should have come in the 1870s, after abundant information about western educational systems was available in the Arab world, is hardly coincidental.[2]

None of these three incidents could have taken place without the prior favorable reports about western accomplishments conveyed by the translators, historians, and travellers of earlier decades. Our concern in this chapter, however, is not with the impact of the information which passed through these sources, but rather with the reactions and attitudes of those who had been responsible for transmitting such information about western accomplishments to the Arab world.

It was perhaps inevitable that the early Arabs who came in contact with the West – whether chroniclers, translators, or travellers – reacted deeply to what they observed or read about the West. Their reactions were significant in two ways. First, many of these attitudes were

1. Ḥ. al-Marṣifi, *al-Kilam al-Thamān fi al-Ummah, al-Waṭan, al-Ḥukūmah, al-ʿAdl, al-Zulm, al-Siyāsah, al-Ḥurrīyah, wa al-Tarbiyah* (The Eight Words – Nation, Patrie, Government, Justice, Injustice, Polity, Freedom and Education), Cairo: 1880.

2. See H. A. R. Gibb, *Modern Trends in Islam*, Chicago: 1947, pp. 39–40. It should be noted that the articles written by Muḥammad ʿAbduh, which appeared in *al-Ahrām* in 1876, called for the inclusion of modern subjects in the Azhar curriculum.

transmitted directly to the reader; and second, their reactions suggest the future reactions of the Arab world, reactions which crystallized during the subsequent period of more intense contact between the two worlds.

This chapter will explore some of the more important attitudes expressed by Arab translators and travellers concerning western accomplishments in the two areas which most attracted their attention, namely, education and the socio-political principles of government. Also considered are the major psychological reactions of the authors to the invidious comparisons they drew between western culture and the contemporary Arab world. Such attitudes and reactions were expressed in different ways. Sometimes they were revealed in the author's attempt to justify his translation or record of his trips. In other cases, they were stated in didactic fashion, a moral being drawn from the presence of something desirable in European culture which was lacking in the Arab world. In still other cases, they were merely reflected in the comments made about a European phenomenon.

Statements of Individual Writers

It will be recalled that Ṭahṭāwi's account of his sojourn in Europe was the first of its kind. He was well aware of the unique task he had set out to perform and thus felt the necessity for justifying his work. The justifications he advanced were quite revealing. Thus, he stated:

> Some of our friends and well-wishers have suggested that I write an account of the strange and foreign things which I observe and come upon … so that it may be beneficial in removing the veil which covers the face of these countries which are said to be the "brides" of all lands … I have urged … the lands of Islam to pursue the foreign [Western] sciences, arts and industries whose perfection in Europe is a well-known and confirmed matter … Throughout my entire stay … I was in extreme agony because of [the contrast between] the French's enjoyment of these things and their absence in the Muslim lands …
>
> And I ask God that this book should meet with favor … and

> that it should awaken the rest of the Islamic nations (*Umam*) from the sleep of ignorance."[1]

Somewhat later in the same book he expressed the hope that

> the fruit of this trip will be realized (God willing) by the spread of these sciences and arts ... by their increased utilization, and by the translating and printing of the books that pertain to them.

And he further stressed that "it is incumbent on the educated to urge all the people to participate in these sciences, arts, and industries."[2]

That this was not only his own view but that of Muḥammad 'Ali as well was emphasized by Ṭahṭāwi when he wrote that the essential reason why Muḥammad 'Ali brought important western scholars to Egypt and sent his student missions abroad was to overcome the abysmal ignorance which prevailed.

> He brought to Egypt every western scholar he could ... and he sent Egyptian students to these countries because their scholars are superior to any others in their learning ... A tradition says that learning is the aim of every believer and that he should seek it even though it may be among the polytheists.[3]

This then was why Ṭahṭāwi wrote his book. He wanted to inform his readers about conditions in Europe as he saw them. And, further, he hoped that his account would induce his Muslim readers to emulate the example of the "unbelievers" in some respects by adopting their basic educational achievements so that the Muslim world would no longer be ignorant.

This idea – that the West far surpassed the Arab world in learning – was repeated throughout Ṭahṭāwi's book. Thus he tells us at one point:

> The European countries have reached the highest stage of

1. Ṭahṭāwi, *Takhlīṣ*, pp. 4, 5. For a fuller discussion of these views in his writings, see A. Amīn, *Fayd al-Khāṭir* (Reflections), Vol. V, Cairo: 1948, pp. 69–91; and A. A. Badawi, *Rifā'ah al-Ṭahṭāwi*, Cairo: 1950, pp. 22–30 and 123–126.
2. Ṭahṭāwi, *Takhlīṣ*, p. 11.
3. *Ibid.*, p. 10.

> perfection in the mathematical sciences, the physical and metaphysical sciences and the branches thereof. Some of them [i.e., European scholars] even participate in the Arabic sciences, even though they have not been guided along the straight path nor have they moved along the road to salvation ... Since the Islamic countries have neglected the intellectual sciences, they stand in need of western countries (*al-Bilād al-Gharbīyah*) to acquire knowledge of which they are ignorant.[1]

A complete enumeration of all the sciences in which Europe surpassed the Arab world was presented by the author. No branch of learning except theology was excluded from Ṭahṭāwi's list. He concluded that: "And if one reflects honestly, one finds that all these sciences are deficient or non-existent in Egypt while the Europeans have perfected them. *And he who is ignorant of something is inferior to him who knows it* ... Thank God who has destined our Benefactor [Muḥammad 'Ali] for our rescue from the darkness of ignorance of all these matters which are known to others."[2]

This problem of ignorance was ever-present in Ṭahṭāwi's thoughts. He recounted, for example, how he was forced to translate a French text on geography in order to teach that subject to his Egyptian students, because no textbook existed in Arabic.[3] And in his introduction to the translation of the Napoleonic Code he justified his labors by saying they were undertaken in order to overcome ignorance:

> This is the translation of a collection of French laws, the codification and writing of which was permitted by the will of the pride of all European Monarchs, Napoleon the First, the Emperor of the French ... [These laws] became very famous subsequently in the European realms ... and they [Europeans] adapted them and took over whatever suited their systems and benefited their relationships with each other ... For this reason the Khedivial Order

1. *Ibid.*, p. 8. See also A. Amīn, *op. cit.*, pp. 106–113; and A. Badawi, *op. cit.*, pp. 128–130; and C. E. Dawn, "From Ottomanism to Arabism," *The Review of Politics*, Vol. XXIII, Notre Dame: 1961, pp. 378–400.
2. Ṭahṭāwi, *Takhlīṣ*, pp. 12, 13. (Italics supplied.)
3. Ṭahṭāwi, *al-Ta'rībāt al-Shāfiyah*, pp. 2–4. See also A. Badawi, *op. cit.*, pp. 153–163.

> to translate them was issued … so that the people of this country will not be ignorant of the principles of European States.[1]

These themes which Ṭahṭāwi stressed appear again and again in the works of other Arabs writing about the West or translating western works during this period. ʿAbduh Khalīfah Maḥmūd justified his translation of the *History of the Reign of the Emperor Charles the Fifth* in the following manner:

> This is a good translation of a comprehensive work elucidating the evolution of society in European countries … Its inclusion in the Arabic language was a most important task, especially in view of the interest shown by the Viceroy in informing himself about such events and his aspirations to educate the people and show them the benefits that may accrue from such learning. For this reason, I translated it.[2]

Maḥmūd had still another intention, which was to present a comparative view of the two societies in both the past and the present. In his own mind there was no doubt that Europe was the center of learning and civilization and that it was because of this that Muslim students were flocking to Europe. It was Maḥmūd's conviction that when those students returned to their own countries, they would again make the Islamic lands the center of civilization they had been in the past.[3]

Bustrus went to Europe initially to recuperate, but he was also "eager to see the Frankish lands noted for their organization and refinement" whose people "are so inclined toward learning and excel in the various arts." Implicit in his account is the hope that his compatriots would compare these achievements with their own and would learn from them.[4]

The motivation for Marrāsh's sojourn in Europe was more

---

1. Ṭahṭāwi, *et al., al-Qānūn al-Faransāwi al-Madani* (The French Civil Code), Cairo: 1866, Vol. 1, pp. 2–3. See also the discussion by A. Badawi, *op. cit.*, pp. 178–180.
2. A. K. Maḥmūd, *Itḥāf al-Mulūk*, Vol. 1, p. 3.
3. *Ibid.* pp. 2–4.
4. Bustrus, *op. cit.*, pp. 1, 54.

explicitly for educational purposes. Disillusioned by the limited scope of education in his native Aleppo and seeking a deeper understanding of the world, he went to Paris specifically to "join its famous school ... and to gain from it the knowledge unobtainable elsewhere." His eloquent descriptions of European progress cannot be understood except in the context of his bitter rejection of the backwardness and corruption he perceived in the Arab world.[1]

Ḥarāyri wrote his booklet in order to explain the principles and rationale of the French trade fairs which, according to him, were held "every ten years so that all the nations (*umam*) can exhibit their products and all the people can see them and learn what each state (*dawlah*) possesses." Noting that the "period of isolation and individuation is ended and everyone tries to learn from others," he advocated Muslim participation in these fairs, recommending that "representatives from all Muslim countries should attend so that they may examine the exhibits and learn what will benefit their countries."[2]

Also convinced of the importance of studying western achievements for internal growth was Khayr al-Dīn. His expressed purpose in writing his book was to "awaken responsible men, statesmen or '*Ulamā*'" to the real situation in both societies. "Thus I have gathered what I could, with God's help, of their innovations in economics and administration, alluding also to their conditions in the past. I have also traced the means whereby they [European countries] have progressed in their political systems to the highest stage." More explicitly, he stated a twofold purpose for his labors.

> The first purpose of this work is to urge those determined and interested (*dhawi al-Ghīrah wa al-hazm*) statesmen and scholars to pursue ... the means which will lead to the welfare of the Islamic nation, and also to seek the means which will lead to the growth of the foundations of Islamic civilization, such as the widening of areas of knowledge and education, the growth of agricultural wealth and of commercial and industrial enterprises ... The basis for all these things is good government, out of which security emerges ... which leads to the perfection of works, as

1. Marrāsh, *Riḥlah*, see pp. 2–9. Quotation from p. 9.
2. Ḥarāyri, *'Arḍ al-Badā' i' al-'Āmm*, Paris: 1867, pp. 2, 4 and 6.

> can be witnessed in the European countries. The second purpose of this work is to warn those ignorant persons among the commonalty of Islam who reject excessively those favorable elements which are possessed by those who do not adhere to our *Sharīʿah* … and who assert that all their [non-believers'] works must be shunned and neglected since their source is evil. *As long as a thing is good in itself, then its source should not deter us from accepting it*; especially so if we already possessed it in the past. Nay, we must retake it and must use it again.

Khayr al-Dīn said that he hoped his discussion of the factors which led to European progress and which were lacking in Islam would influence the responsible authorities to "select those means which are suitable to our own case, and which are compatible with our own *Sharīʿah*. In this way we may be freed from our present dilemmas."[1] Thus, Khayr al-Dīn gave his comprehensive account of the development and evolution of European society in order to demonstrate clearly – by its contrast with contemporary Arab society – the ascendency of Europe at that particular moment. This he accomplished by the traditional technique of stating his point and then alluding to an event in Islamic history or a line from Arabic literature for supporting evidence.

It should be noted that Khayr al-Dīn stressed the basic superiority of western culture primarily in non-military terms. Although he alluded to the military impregnability of Europe, he also pointed out that this ascendency was attained only after their progress in intellectual affairs and hence was not independent of those achievements. Military power was merely an outgrowth of the two essential principles upon which the strength of any society must depend, that is, freedom and political justice. It was to the development of these two principles that he attributed European advances and it was these same principles he advocated being incorporated into Islamic society.[2]

Europe's progress and her superiority in practically all fields of knowledge and achievement continued to be lauded in even more

1. Khayr al-Dīn, *Aqwam al-Masālik fi Maʿrifat Ahwāl al-Mamālik*, Tunis: 1867, quotations are taken from pp. 4–6. (Italics supplied.)
2. *Ibid.*, pp. 20–22; See also A. Amīn, *op. cit.*, Vol. VI, 1945. pp. 212–216.

extreme terms by the travellers who found their way to her shores after the mid-century. One of these later travellers, Muḥammad Bayram, who made repeated trips to Europe between 1867 and 1886, affirmed the superiority of European medical knowledge implicitly, for he travelled to Europe for medical treatment unavailable elsewhere.[1]

His reason for going to Europe may have been his health, but Bayram returned to his home with more than an improved physique. He returned to write a five-volume geopolitical study of the Europe he visited. In it, in addition to constant allusions to freedom and justice, he included detailed and comprehensive physical descriptions of what he had observed. He described the libraries, the industries, agriculture, means of communication and travel, as well as the political system of each country and its historical development. After each glowing description, he deplored the deficiencies in the Muslim world which suffered through contrast.[2]

A similar desire to convey to Arab readers the "strange and wondrous things in the West" was felt by Muḥammad Amīn Fikri, who went to Europe in 1889 as a delegate to the Orientalist Congress in Stockholm. In the introduction to his book he indicated that the purpose of his narration was to aid his countrymen by giving them an account of the things he saw in Europe which they might consider emulating.[3]

In general, the conclusions reached by these culture carriers was that Europe had outdistanced the Islamic world in the broad field of learning and in the more specific field of political organization. In fact, the advances in the latter area – because they were based upon freedom and political justice – facilitated the free pursuit of knowledge and the development of industries which gave Europe her ascendency. The writers deplored, explicitly or implicitly, the lack of such advances in their own world.

---

1. Muḥammad Bayram, *Ṣafwat al-I'tibār bi Mustawda' al-Amṣār wa al-Aqṭār*, Cairo: 1884–1886, Vol. 1, pp. 15–16. See also Zaydān, *Ta'rīkh* pp. 215–216.
2. Actually, only three of the five volumes were devoted to Europe itself. For some illustrations of his method, see Bayram, *op. cit.*, Vol. III, pp. 6–28, 34–36.
3. M. A. Fikri, *Irshād al-Alibbā' ila Maḥāsin Ūrubba*, Cairo: 1892, pp. 1–9. Also Zaydān, *Ta'rīkh*, pp. 190–191.

Mere acknowledgement of the superior qualities of another culture, however, may lead to varied reactions. Observers may react by abandoning their entire cultural heritage in an attempt to emulate what they deem to be the superior culture. With greater caution and moderation they may urge the selective adoption of some but not all elements of the other culture. Or, from fear and defensiveness, they may build elaborate rationalizations for the failure of their own culture and vehemently reject the foreign culture as undesirable. During the nineteenth century, this entire gamut of response to western culture was expressed.

Reactions to the Invidious Comparisons

The first important reaction of Arab "rediscoverers" of nineteenth-century Europe was that of selective adoption. They suggested that the Muslim world ought to accept and adapt certain beneficial aspects of western culture, but only when the adaptation could be made within the framework of the legal and moral system of the *Sharī'ah*. This obviously left the matter somewhat indeterminate, since what was or was not compatible with the Islamic legal framework was scarcely a settled and unequivocal fact. In addition, this position tended to ignore the interrelatedness of cultural traits and the unforeseen consequences which might be set in motion by a seemingly simple and limited change.

The proponents of this view seem to have been blithely unaware of these implications. Ṭahṭāwi hints that complete confidence in "rationality" might be somewhat incompatible with the *Sharī'ah* when he criticizes what he considered to be the excessive French belief in this method of knowledge to the exclusion of divine revelation.[1] But he did not make this explicit nor did he elaborate on this point. Whether or not he perceived a potential threat to Islam from this source cannot be ascertained. He did urge the pursuit of all branches of western learning – including the pure sciences, philosophy, politics, history, economics, and administration – in addition

1. Ṭahṭāwi, *Takhlīṣ*, p. 22.

to the fields of utilitarian technology.[1] If he feared "rationality", it is unlikely that he would have been so unselective.

Coupled with this desire to learn from the West was the attitude that such learning was well within the realm of possibility for the Arabs. The writers emphasized that Europe had not always enjoyed the scientific ascendency and temporal power that were hers at that particular point in history. It was repeatedly explained to Muslim readers that Europe had undergone a series of historical developments, had passed through several historical stages which were not dissimilar from those through which Islamic society had passed.

Several authors followed a basic fourfold division in their analysis of western history. According to their narration, the first stage was the barbaric era that preceded the rise of Greek civilization. This was followed by a second stage characterized by enlightenment and progress in all aspects of knowledge except those pertaining to the unity of God. This second period closed in 476 A.D. when the new barbarians invaded the crumbling Roman Empire. The third stage was a return to relative ignorance, although learning was kept alive in the monasteries where it was restricted to the clergy. This period was followed by the fourth and most recent stage, which began with the Renaissance of the fifteenth and sixteenth centuries. (The authors mentioned the earlier eleventh-century renaissance but, perhaps understandably, did not stress its importance.) This final period was characterized by vigorous intellectual and material progress throughout western Europe. It was during this period that the center of civilization began to move away from the Muslim lands to the European countries.

The advances in the West at that period were not easily won, however. The rulers of Europe were not concerned with the welfare of their subjects but sought only to restrict and abuse them. The people suffered but struggled, often with bloodshed, to improve their lot, Only occasionally were they aided by enlightened monarchs. But their struggle was successful, and finally, after a long and gradual

1. *Ibid.*, pp. 259–262.

process of evolution and at some points revolution. Europe arrived at her present stage of civilization.

Two main conclusions were drawn from this historical approach: first, that "civilization" is merely a stage in temporal development and not a sign of inherent superiority; and second, the people must want and be willing to sacrifice in order to reach such an enviable position.[1]

Europe's ultimate success in achieving her present ascendency was attributed by these authors to three main causes. First, the Europeans had shown great initiative and vitality. Second, they had gradually evolved a sound political system based upon freedom and political justice. And third – and perhaps of utmost importance to these writers – the Europeans had been willing to profit from their contact with Muslim peoples, a contact that was negative, as in the Crusades, as well as positive, as in Spain and Italy. The Europeans had learned many things from the Muslims in all aspects of knowledge and thus were able to advance their society. They were able to profit from their contact with Islamic lands only because they were open-minded, that is, because they were willing to learn whatever they considered valuable from others, even from those whose religious affiliation differed from their own.[2]

The authors drew certain morals from their analysis. They believed first of all that Muslims should not be discouraged by the superficial dissimilarities between Europe and their own lands. Muslims could, if they wished, gain a position of equality *vis-à-vis* Europe. In order to achieve that end, however, it was necessary for them to revitalize their creativity, to be willing to learn from the West, and to change their system of political authority.

A second lesson they drew was that, just as retrogression and reaction had occurred in the once vital Muslim world, so the same latent forces of decay were present in Europe. Only intellectual and political vigilance could keep European culture at its present pinnacle. Clearly,

---

1. This general historical approach was followed by A. K. Maḥmūd, *Itḥāf al-Mulūk*, pp. 4–10; by Khayr al-Dīn, *op. cit.*, pp. 51–55; and by Muḥammad Bayram, *op. cit.*, Vol. 1, pp. 41–43.

2. Ṭahṭāwi, *Takhlīṣ*, pp. 8, 79–96; Khayr al-Dīn, *op. cit.*, pp. 51 ff.; and M. Bayram, *op. cit.*, Vol. 1, pp. 43–45.

the intention of the Arab authors was to prove that neither society was inherently superior or inferior. And, in at least one aspect of culture, the Muslim world was more fortunate than Europe because of its superior religion. (We will return to this point later.)

To what extent did the authors who took the position that Muslims must learn from the West see any limitations to this process? Did they prefer certain branches of knowledge to others and did they proscribe the study of any fields of European knowledge? As far as can be determined from their writings, no. All western fields except theology were recommended for study. Only Ṭahṭāwi expressed any reservations, and even he recommended caution rather than abstinence. When describing the philosophy of the French, he warned his readers that

> Some of the ideas in philosophy and related sciences are misleading since they contradict *all* Divine Books ... [The French philosophers] marshall a great deal of evidence in support of their contentions, and this evidence is very difficult to refute ... Let it be said that their philosophy books are filled with a great many innovations ... and thus, anyone wishing to study French philosophical works must be extremely well-versed in the Book [*Qur'ān*] and the *Tradition* if his beliefs are not to be undermined. Otherwise he might lose his faith.[1]

This statement was the only dissenting view concerning indiscriminate study of western subjects. It is significant that Ṭahṭāwi did not tell his readers to eschew entirely the study of philosophy; he merely warned them of the possible repercussions which such study might have on minds untutored in traditional Islamic studies.

While, on the whole, reactions to Europe were positive and accepting, it was perhaps natural that the early writers and travellers should also feel somewhat defensive. Conscious of the unequal status of the two societies, they attempted to retrieve some vestige of ego by apologetics. Admittedly, these early apologetics were in embryonic form but they foreshadowed a reaction which was to become a

1. Ṭahṭāwi, *Takhlīṣ*, p. 153.

dominant response of Arabs to western culture.[1] In a highly perceptive comment on the state of mind which led to this defensiveness, H. A. R. Gibb has written,

> Even those conservative Moslems who seek for encouragement or example in their own past and who relate incidents in early Islamic history to show that the principles and qualities sought today are to be found in their own tradition, consciously or unconsciously select those instances which accord with the western point of view, and neglect all that too sharply contrasts with it.[2]

The defensiveness of early students of the West revealed itself in a number of ways. The first and most apparent manifestation was in political theory. It will be recalled that the Arab authors were greatly impressed by constitutionalism and the representative nature of European governments, both of which were noticeably lacking in the Muslim world. Because the authors wanted to see this system in their own society, they claimed, rightly or wrongly, that it was the natural form of government in Islam. They claimed that the principle of *al-shūra* (consultation) implied parliamentary government. It was noted that originally the Caliphs had followed the example of Muḥammad and abided by this principle, and that only subsequently and gradually did it fall into neglect. Exactly how the principle fell into disuse was not made clear by the authors, but Khayr al-Dīn stressed that it followed (1) the split of the Islamic State into the 'Abbāsid, Fāṭimid, and Umayyad components, and (2) the Mongol invasion. He was unwilling to commit himself, however, to the proposition that the principle of *al-shūra* was applied consistently before that time.

Another line of argument attempting to prove that constitutionalism was inherent in Islam was that one of the most important

1. Later developments in apologetics are discussed by Gustave E. von Grunebaum in *Approaches to Group Understanding*, ed. L. Bryson, *et al.*, New York: 1947, pp. 785–820. See also his article, "The Problem of Cultural Influence," in *Charisteria Orientalia*, ed. Felix Tauer, *et al.*, Prague: 1956, pp. 86–99; and W. C. Smith, *Islam in Modern History*, Princeton: 1957, pp. 115–160.
2. H. A. R. Gibb, ed., *Whither Islam?*, London: 1932, p. 320.

characteristics of the *Sharīʿah* was the controls and limits it imposed upon rulers to prevent absolute power by any man. That is, they contended that the *Qurʾān* and the *Tradition* were sufficient instruments to bring about a government of law, if only they were followed.[1] In fact, one writer even went so far in apologetics as to claim that the Muslim world had never lost its constitutional basis because it still adhered to the *Qurʾān* and the *Tradition*. This same man contended that the reason why Europe had to struggle to achieve her representative institutions of government was precisely because she lacked the *Sharīʿah*. Since neither the European people nor their monarchs had been graced by Divine Revelation, Europe's transition from an absolute form of government to that of a representative one could only be achieved through struggle, a struggle which presumably was unnecessary in Islam.[2]

What is most impressive about this early response was the alacrity with which the authors subscribed to the underlying principles of western institutions of government. Even their attempt to retrace them to an Islamic origin indicates a readiness to accept and assimilate western political ideology, a readiness not completely obscured by their somewhat tenuous arguments.

Apologetics were not confined to politics but extended into other areas as well. Nineteenth-century Arab westernizers explicitly acknowledged the superiority of Europe in the sciences and the arts. This forced them again to look backward to the time when the Muslim world had excelled in scholarship while Europe was "in the

1. R. R. Ṭahṭāwi, *Manāhij al-Albāb al-Miṣrīyah fi Mabāhij al-ādāb al-ʿAṣrīyah* (Courses for Egyptian Minds in the Delights of Modern Literatures), Cairo: 1912 edition, pp. 323 and 437; A. K. Maḥmūd, *op. cit.*, Vol. III, p. 357; Khayr al-Dīn, *op. cit.*, pp. 20–22, 30–33. For some illustrations of later developments of this theme, i.e. constitutionalism in Islam, see A. R. Kawākibi, *Umm al-Qura* (Metropolis), Cairo: 1931, pp. 58, 194–195; and his *Ṭabāʾiʿ al-Istibdād*, Cairo: 1905, pp. 22–26. See also R. Riḍa, ed., *Taʾrīkh al-Ustādh al-lmām al-Shaykh Muḥammad ʿAbduh* (A Biography of Muhammad ʿAbduh), Vol. II, Cairo: 1926, pp. 52–54, 92–98, 197–205.

2. Maḥmūd, *Itḥāf al-Mulūk*, Vol. III, pp. 357–359. This argument was in rebuttal to W. Robertson's indictment of the Ottoman Sultan as an autocrat who had no responsibility to any representative assembly capable of restraining his actions. Maḥmūd's translation of Robertson's text contains an appendix in which the translator "corrects" misrepresentations in the text.

grip of the most horrible form of savagery and barbarism."[1] The writers emphasized the previous role of the Muslim world as the center of learning and civilization. A few quotations may demonstrate how this line of defense was utilized in early nineteenth-century Arabic literature. Ṭahṭāwi wrote,

> We were, at the time of the Caliphs, the most perfect of all countries. The reason for this was that the Caliphs used to patronize the scholars and learned men, the artists and other worthy persons. Some of the Caliphs even occupied themselves with such pursuits ... From this one knows that learning does not spread in any era except through the support of the State.[2]

Maḥmūd, in the introduction to his translation, wrote in a similar vein: "The Muslim lands used to be the center for learning and the sciences, but ... then a period of decline set in ... In the meantime, Europe gradually emerged from its age of ignorance through its contact with the Islamic people ... until it became the new center of civilization, learning and the sciences. Muslims recognize this and are trying to rectify their own situation by sending students to Europe and by translating European works."[3]

Khayr al-Dīn made a similar point in stating that:

> From what we have said earlier, one can learn the extent of the growth of Islamic civilization, of its wealth and military prowess. All of this was the outcome of justice and unity and the brotherhood which existed in the various Islamic states, and of the utmost attention which all of them paid to learning, science and other related subjects then prevalent in Islam. These things the Europeans emulated, and those fair-minded men among them testify that the Islamic nation deserves the credit for the present progress in all these disciplines.[4]

To support his last statement about "fair-minded" Europeans who "testify" to Muslim contributions, Khayr al-Dīn translated an entire

1. This phrase is translated directly from Khayr al-Dīn, *op. cit.*, p. 9.
2. Ṭahṭāwi, *Takhlīṣ*, p. 9.
3. A. K. Maḥmūd, *Itḥāf al-Mulūk*, Vol. I, pp. 2–4.
4. Khayr al-Dīn, *op. cit.*, p. 29.

section of Jean Victor Duruy's *Histoire du Moyen-Age* (which he identified only by the last name of the author), dealing with Islamic civilization. The opening paragraph indicated why Khayr al-Dīn found it expedient to translate this portion of Duruy's work.

> *En effet, tandis que l'Europe était plongée dans ténèbres de barbarie que percèrent à peine quelques faibles lueurs, une vive lumière de littérature, de philosophie, de science, d'arts, d'industrie inondait toutes les capitales de l'islamisme. Bagdad, Bassorah, Samarcande, Damas, le Caire, Kairoan, Fez, Grenade, Cordoueétaient autant de grands centres intellectuels.*[1]

Duruy's testimony was frequently cited by Khayr al-Dīn to support his view that "we were their masters and mentors" in all fields of knowledge.

The authors deplored the fact that this brilliant epoch of Islamic history had passed away and that political justice and freedom were lost in the Islamic lands when the Islamic nation was divided into numerous rival states. Implicit in their analysis is the prescription that unity, political justice, and freedom would permit a return to previous Islamic glory.

Not only did Arab writers draw solace from the image of past achievements but they also used these past accomplishments to minimize to some extent the uniqueness and independence of western gains. Not only did they claim that the Muslims were the original masters and benefactors, but they implied that the present state of European progress could never have been achieved had it not been for the earlier Muslim civilization. There is little doubt that this early line of reasoning presaged the apologetics which pervade contemporary Arabic literature.

Still another modern response, apologetic in character, was discernible in the nineteenth century, i.e. the greater spirituality of the East as a compensation for its lack of material advance. It was in the writings of Jamāl al-Dīn al-Afghāni (1839–1897) that the now

---

1. We have traced this quotation to J. V. Duruy, *Histoire du Moyen-Age*, Paris: 1880, 10th edition, p. 122 ff. The Arabic translation of this passage appears in Khayr al-Dīn, *op. cit.*, pp. 22–31.

accepted dichotomy between *al-Islām wa al-Gharb* (Islam and the West) received its earliest systematic treatment.[1] Since that time the concept has become an accepted part of Arab dogma and is in constant currency in Arabic literature. The dichotomy which al-Afghāni sharpened and crystallized, however, had already been suggested by earlier Arab writers.

In the writings of Ṭahṭāwi, for example, the phrase *al-Bilād al-Gharbīyah* appears, apparently for the first time in Arabic literature, to denote the West, as opposed to the world of Islam. He tried to convey the basic view that there were two worlds, *al-Bilād al-Islāmīyah* (Islamic countries) and *al-Bilād al-Gharbīyah* (western countries), each of which possessed different but complementary attributes. Whereas Muslims possessed the *Sharī' ah*, the distinguishing characteristic of their culture, the West was distinguished by its possession of scientific knowledge.[2] In this attempt to distinguish between the basic elements of the two cultures can be found the first hint of the dichotomy between the spiritual East and the materialistic West. In another part of his work, Ṭahṭāwi described the French as materialists who love the pursuit of material wealth, being very unlike the Arabs in this respect.[3]

An even more explicit statement of the relative virtues of the two cultures was made by the translator 'Abduh Khalifah Maḥmūd, who stated:

> God ... honored Asia with the pride of the Message, the Prophethood, Generosity and Chivalry (*Futuwwah*) ... Then He bestowed upon Europe the pride of the utilitarian sciences and the arts of brilliant education. He moved the Europeans from the

1. Jamāl al-Dīn al-Afghāni and Muḥammad 'Abduh, *Al-'Urwah al-Wuthqa* (The Indissoluble Bond), Cairo: 1928, pp. 30–45, 61–72; M. al-Makhzūmi, *Khāṭirāt Jamāl al-Dīn al-Afghāni* (Reflections of Jamāl al-Dīn al-Afghāni), Cairo: 1931, pp. 141–145, 449–460. For a brief account of al-Afghāni's life and labors in awakening the Muslim world, see E. G. Browne, *The Persian Revolution*, London: 1909, Chapter 1; I. Goldziher, "Djamāl al-Dīn al-Afghāni," in *Encyclopedia of Islam*, Vol. 1, pp. 1008–11; C. C. Adams, *Islam and Modernism in Egypt*, London: 1933, pp. 4–17; J. Zaydān, *Tarājim Mashāhīr*, Vol. II, pp. 52–61; and A. Amīn, *Zu'amā'*, pp. 59–121.
2. See above, p. 145.
3. Ṭahṭāwi, *Ṭakhlīṣ*, pp. 139–140; A. Amīn, *Fayd*, p. 82.

> era of uncouthness to civilization and He made them the masters of sciences and industries ...[1]

Therefore, by the middle of the nineteenth century the theory that there was a "division of labor" or specialization between cultures – a Spiritual East and a Materialistic West – had already been expressed in embryonic form. Later eastern writers and reformers, Muslim and non-Muslim alike, were to belabor and exhaust this theme.[2]

1. A. K. Maḥmūd, *Itḥaf al-Mulūk*, p. 2.
2. See Ṭāha Ḥusayn, *Mustaqbal al-Thaqāfah*, Cairo: 1938, pp. 65–70, English translation, pp. 20–22. See also A. Amīn, *Fayḍ*, Vol. II, pp. 52–59.

EIGHT

Conclusions and Subsequent Developments

The Arabs of the nineteenth century had come a long way between 1798 and 1870. In the eighteenth century they had been almost totally isolated from the main stream of world events; by 1870 their involvement with at least western Europe was a *fait accompli*, manifested not only in their concrete knowledge of the West but, even more important, in their eager interest in and emulation of western European developments.

These extremes – ignorance of the West on the one hand and knowledge and interest on the other – are perhaps best illustrated by two figures, each of whom was a product as well as a shaper of his era. First, one has the account of the Egyptian historian, 'Abd al-Raḥmān al-Jabarti, in which he displayed an almost total ignorance of the background of the European forces whose occupation of Egypt he described. Compare this with a weekly magazine, *al-Jinān*, which in 1870 devoted half of its issues to European events. The editor and publisher of this journal, Buṭrus al-Bustāni, was perhaps personally interested in these events, but that he could have devoted so much of his publication to events on other continents also reflects the widened interests of his readers.

During this same year a number of books on European history were written (not translated) by Arabs. The subsequent publication of these books indicates the extent to which awareness of, interest in, and involvement with the West had become an integral part of the Arab cultural milieu. Significantly, this was the time when more traditionally oriented members of the Arab intelligentsia began to castigate the younger generation for their excessive "westernization."[1]

Knowledge and involvement had not developed in a vacuum. Much of the ground was prepared during the earliest phase of westernization, which we have dated between 1800 and 1870. It is necessary to distinguish clearly between the pre-1870 and post-1870 phases of westernization, since each was characterized by distinctly different processes. Before analyzing the differences, however, we might summarize here the major characteristics of the first phase of cultural contact between the Arab and western worlds, as they appear from the foregoing study.

During this initial phase, the major agents of change and the more important transmitters of culture seem to have been endogenous. Much of the progress in westernization between 1800 and 1870 was accomplished through the administrative and literary efforts of Arabs who were in direct or indirect contact with the West. The image they had formed of the West was communicated to their compatriots, at least in part, through their writings. Many of these writers were deeply influenced by their contact and not only described the West but exhorted their compatriots to follow its example. Thus, the translators of European books, the authors of travel accounts about Europe, and the "historians" of western culture constituted a major force guiding Arab society toward westernization. To point to their contribution, however, is not to minimize or deny the existence of exogenous forces as well. These were also important; however, their role during the first phase of culture contact was somewhat secondary to that of native westernizers, particularly in comparison with a later stage of the process.

---

1. In addition to the remarks of Bustāni (see above, p. 141), Nawfal Ni'mat Allah al-Ṭarābulsi also admonished the Lebanese youth of his time for relying on Voltaire. He stated, "Few are those who have any confidence in the works of this man. Unfortunately, however, we find a large number of our youth who have learned foreign languages alleging that all their education is without value unless they have avidly read his and other similar works so as to follow in his footsteps and be in the avant-guarde of the civilized (*muta-maddinīn*)." See his *Zubdat al-Ṣaḥā' if fi Uṣūl al-Ma'ārif* (Best Pages in the Foundation of Knowledge), Beirut: 1874, Vol. II, pp. 427–428.

A second major characteristic of the initial phase of contact was the kind of "image" of the West held up to view. For the most part, Arabs of 1870 subscribed to a favorable image of the West which had been nurtured by earlier writers of chronicles, translators of western books, and authors of travel accounts. By that time and on the strength of that image, an important segment of Arab intellectual leadership was seeking reforms in their own society to make it more similar to Europe. While it is perhaps impossible at this date to portray the exact nature of the image held by nineteenth-century Arabs, a tentative reformulation of the image is possible, utilizing the sources which have been analyzed in the preceding chapters.

From these works it is evident that certain Arabs of the nineteenth century had developed a deep respect for the multifaceted achievements of western society, particularly in three major areas. First, Europe was admired for having evolved a sound political system. The principles of European ideology singled out for particular commendation by the Arab writers were: constitutionalism, especially with reference to limitations on the absolute power of the executive branch; freedom, both of the individual and of association; and justice. These were considered the underlying causes of Europe's political and social "health."

Second, Arabs of the nineteenth century attributed the vitality and "progressiveness" of Europe to its educational system and its social organization. Recognized as important prerequisites to western accomplishment were a spirit of free inquiry, and educational and scholarly institutions supported but not controlled by the state. The contribution of private organizations and associations to the economic and humanitarian advances of Europe was also acknowledged.

And third, Arabs were coming to appreciate the literary expression of western society, independent of its utilitarian value. This interest led them to translate significant "humanist" literature which ultimately assumed an importance out of proportion to its quantity.

This image of the West was obviously more comprehensive than has hitherto been assumed. A number of scholars have claimed that nineteenth-century Arabs were interested almost exclusively in the techniques and technology of the West. Furthermore, it has been suggested that their preoccupation with technical and military affairs was motivated, in the words of Arnold Toynbee, by a desire to westernize "as a means toward their becoming more competent to hold their own against Western Imperialism."[1] While this may have been true of Muhammad 'Ali himself, it should not be generalised to an entire cultural response. Our facts suggest that certain Arabs during the first phase of westernization saw much more in the West than its techniques and military machine. Quite properly, they recognized the latter as by-products of more fundamental characteristics and, where they advocated reform, did so not in the technological sphere but in the realms of politics, education, social organization, and literature.

Implicit or explicit in their writings is an acknowledgement of western superiority in all spheres except the religious. They called upon their compatriots to examine western culture objectively and to adopt those elements which would spark an evolution within their own society. But they also recommended adapting the change to the framework of their own cultural values, i.e. within the *Sharīah*. Unfortunately, they seem to have been only vaguely aware that this could not always be done, and hence offered no hints as to which western elements might prove most incompatible with existing moral values.

Together with this acknowledgement of superiority, however, went a defensiveness and what we have termed elsewhere the beginnings of Arab "apologetics." Because the West lacked the Divine Revelation, it was inferior to the East spiritually, although it exceeded the latter in other realms of life. Furthermore, even those elements in western life singled out for special commendation – such as constitutionalism, representative government, justice – were viewed not as traits inherent in western society but achievements gained only after much bloodshed and violence. Since, during the "Golden Age of Islam," the East had already attained these values, Muslims were

1. Arnold Toynbee, *A Study of History*, Vol. VIII, London: 1954, p. 692. See also pp. 216–272 of the same volume.

exhorted to adopt and adapt from Europe in order to return to the principles that underlay early Islamic society. Thus, both doctrines – the juxta-position of a spiritual East and a materialist West and the urge to revive the Golden Age of Islam – emerged at this time as defensive reactions to acknowledged western superiority.

This brings us to the third characteristic of early westernization – that it was advocated primarily by Muslims, a fact often overlooked because it was soon obscured by later developments. The image of the West described above was created chiefly by deeply religious Muslims. The fact that Europe was a Christian society neither deterred them from acknowledging her superiority nor prevented them from advocating the adoption of many of her basic features. At no point during this early phase of Arab-western contact did Arabs seem to view Europe as a secular society. They may have deplored her misguided religion, and they certainly condemned her tendency toward "backsliding"; but rather than being attracted by her secularism they failed even to perceive it. Perhaps the concept that any society *could* be secular was too bizarre to be comprehended.

The final characteristic of this first phase of Arab-European contact is its geographic locus. It has been suggested by many that western influence and the transmission of western ideas to the Arab world was largely a Lebanese contribution.[1] Historically speaking, however, Egypt seems to have played a more basic role during the earliest epoch, administratively, institutionally, and culturally. While the administrative and institutional aspects of westernization have not been dealt with in this book, our examination of the transmission of western ideas and of the growth of Arab awareness of the West suggests that Egypt was the significant center of the movement during the first seven decades of the nineteenth century. During that period, translations of western books were made first in Egypt. Only later did they appear in the Lebanon. Examination of the bibliography included in the text demonstrates that the largest majority of publications

1. This suggestion was carefully examined by N. A. Faris in his "Lebanon, 'Land of Light,'" in J. Kritzeck and R. B. Winder, *The World of Islam*, London: 1960, pp. 336–350. A conclusion similar to ours was reached.

contributing significantly to a growing Arab awareness of the West had in fact come out of Egypt.

These are, briefly stated, the major characteristics of the first phase of contact between the two cultures. The relatively few forces at work during the first period were eventually drowned out by a flood of objective changes in the local environment which accelerated the pace of westernization. Elements of these objective forces began to appear with increasing frequency during the second half of the nineteenth century, until by 1870 the network was so complex that the nature of the process of change itself underwent a transformation.

Muḥammad ʿAli's early efforts to westernize his country were in most instances frustrated, but the projects first conceived under him were eventually brought to fruition by his successors. Thus, major rail lines, proposed originally during his time, were finally executed under Saʾīd (1854–1863). Cotton raised for export, another innovation of Muḥammad ʿAli, drew Egypt increasingly into the instabilities and interdependencies of the world market, particularly during the American Civil War when she became the most important substitute source of supply for the mills of England and the continent. The Suez Canal, long suggested as a possibility, was finally opened in 1869, thus linking irrevocably the fate and prosperity of Egypt with the strategies of Europe.

No longer could Egypt sit at leisure and voluntarily sample or reject western developments. The presence of increasing numbers of European individuals and firms and their growing influence over Khedivial decisions, plus the changes which resulted from the new technologies, removed the option. Each increase in westernization seemed to breed the need for more. Finally, the power to opt was removed entirely, as the bankruptcy of the country led to the deposing of Khedive Ismāʾīl in 1879 and the ultimate occupation of Egypt by Britain (1882). Exogenous forces of westernization had achieved primacy in the process.

Developments in the Fertile Crescent, while they did not parallel those in Egypt, took the same general direction. Exogenous influences were becoming more important. Foreign missionaries, who had initially come to the area as early as the eighteenth century, began in the nineteenth to widen their sphere of activities. During the first half of that century they opened elementary schools; after mid-century their efforts culminated in the establishment of two institutions of higher learning in Beirut: the Syrian Protestant College (now American University of Beirut) established in 1866; and the University of St. Joseph, founded in 1874.[1] Other foreigners, less well-intentioned, had taken advantage of the tangled affairs of the Levant to become partners of the Porte in the administration of the Lebanon. Thus, in the Fertile Crescent no less than in Egypt, westerners themselves – working as educators, administrators, or in commercial and technical capacities – were assuming more and more the burden of bringing about change.

But just as foreigners had been active during the first phase of westernization, so did Arabs participate in this second phase. In the period just after 1870, Arabs in increasing numbers were calling for reforms of all kinds. Their demands, although never embodied in a coherent or comprehensive program, were reasonably articulate.[2] The reforms were to be modelled on the western example; and the more these reforms were urged, the more pressing became the need to acquire further knowledge of the prototype.

1. L. Shaykhu, in his examination of the contribution of foreign missionaries and the growth of their activities, has stressed these changes in educational material and missionary publications. See his *al-Ādāb al-'Arabīyah fi al-Qarn al-Tāsi' 'Ashar*, Vol. II, pp. 3–8. See also *al-Mashriq*, Beirut: 1908, pp. 774–782. Many chroniclers of modern Arab developments have explored the contributions of foreign missionaries to the general cultural revival of the Arab world. See, for example, P. K. Hitti, *History of Syria*, New York: 1951, pp. 611–616; G. Antonius, *The Arab Awakening*, Philadelphia: 1939, pp. 35–45; and Z. N. Zeine, *Arab-Turkish Relations and the Rise of Arab Nationalism*, Beirut: 1958, pp. 42–45. For some idea of the American missionary schools in Syria prior to the establishment of the American University, see H. H. Jessup, *Fifty-Three Years in Syria*, Boston: 1910, Vol. II, pp. 805–815. For similar schools in Egypt, see J. Heyworth-Dunne, *An Introduction*, pp. 333, 406, 410–412, 415. Other good accounts of the role of the American University at Beirut can be found in S. Penrose, *That They May Have Life; the Story of the American University of Beirut*, 1866–1941, New York: 1941; and Bayard Dodge, *The American University of Beirut*, Beirut: 1958.

2. This was the age of Jamāl al-Dīn al-Afghāni, Muḥammad 'Abduh, Adīb Isḥāq, and Kawākibi, among others.

It was at this time that increasing numbers of translations from European works were made, not under governmental auspices but by private individuals trying to meet an existing demand. The great variety of books translated after 1870 reflects the broader cultural ambitions of the period. Original works about the West, which were neither translations nor travel accounts, also began to appear, reflecting increased mastery of both the languages of the West and the content of its culture. Travel to Europe increased perceptibly in the post-1870 period, resulting in broadened knowledge and a proliferation of new travel accounts. By this time the Lebanon had come to play a more active role in the movements of reform and westernization, outdistancing the other center at Cairo.

During this period of increased activity, Arab awareness of the West expanded and deepened. In the Arabic literature of the first part of the nineteenth century, it is obvious that awareness of the West meant, for all practical purposes, awareness of France. France was the model. Knowledge of the rest of Europe was gained through French eyes. Translations from western literature were confined to French originals, while descriptions of that country absorbed most of the travel books.

During the second phase of westernization, other countries were, in effect, "discovered." The presence of English, American, German, and Italian personnel and businessmen in the Middle East contributed to that discovery, as did a widening of the travel itineraries of individual Arabs. Travel accounts dealt with a variety of countries, and translations from English, German and, later, American and Russian literature began to appear after 1870. This new knowledge increased the variety and confusion of "western" models. The model was no longer post-revolutionary France. Conflicting ideologies and systems – drawn from England, the United States, Germany, Italy, and Russia – gave to late westernization its somewhat eclectic pattern.

During the second phase of westernization, along with changes in personnel and image, a parallel change in technology occurred which served to broaden the impact of western influence. This was the emergence of a popular Arabic press. With the gradual increase in the literacy rate, the presses of Cairo and Beirut began to affect a somewhat wider audience than had been reached during the first phase of westernization.

A final comment must be made on another major characteristic of the second phase of the Arab-western encounter. It was during this second period that a decidedly hostile reaction to western phenomena began to spread. It seemed to grow at a rate which corresponded to the accelerating pace of westernization and involvement with the West. While this is not the place to trace the development and manifestations of this reaction, it may be suggested by the increased tempo of change, to a realization of the actual and potential threats such changes raised to traditional social and cultural values (which had been only vaguely sensed during the earlier phase), as well as to the very real fact of spreading western occupation.[1]

The end of this second phase of Arab response to the West is impossible to fix with any precision, and certainly the individual Arab states have been emerging from it at different rates and from different starting points. We would suggest that the end of World War II, when the Arab states began gradually to acquire real as well as nominal independence and autonomy, marks the beginning of a new phase in the process of westernization. Initiative has again returned to endogenous agents of change and reform – but in a much altered world.

This primacy of endogenous forces of westernization makes the third phase of the cultural encounter more akin to the first than to the second. During the present phase, however, the native agents of change are themselves westernized. The majority are products of western institutions of higher learning, either in the Middle East or abroad. The remainder have been educated in national educational institutions; but these institutions were so transformed during the second phase of westernization that their graduates are "westernized" indirectly. It is almost impossible to speak of recent Arab political and intellectual leadership outside these two main sources.

1. See the interesting remarks of M. K. 'Ayyad, "The Future of Culture in Arab Society," in Walter Laqueur, ed., *The Middle East in Transition*, New York: 1958, pp. 462–477.

Another parallel between the first and third periods of culture contact is the almost dizzying rate at which western books – European and American – are now being translated into Arabic. These new translations, undertaken for different purposes than during the first phase, reflect increased sophistication and critical facility. The quantity of translation which has been undertaken outside government auspices indicates the existence of a fairly extensive and responsive mass audience for western books.[1]

The multitude of contemporary travel accounts offers a third parallel. The travel of students, official missions, and private individuals to western countries has increased to such an extent that sheer numbers have become meaningless. Muḥammad 'Ali's first student missions (1809–1826) involved twenty-eight persons; in 1960, a not exceptional year, the Egyptian government alone sent more than one thousand students abroad for higher training. More travel books about the West have been published in the past decade than appeared during the preceding century and a half. In quality they are infinitely superior, being more informative and reflecting a broader background and a greater familiarity.

Two additional characteristics of this third and contemporary phase of westernization distinguish it drastically from those

1. During the past ten years, a wide variety of western books has become available in translation. Not only the older classics of Locke, Hobbes, Hume. Voltaire, and Rousseau but the more recent contributions of Marx and Engels, Freud, John Dewey, Laski, Toynbee, Camus, Sartre, O'Neil, Hemingway, Sarton, and W. Rostow, to mention but a few, have been translated in this new burst of energy. Translations, acknowledged and unacknowledged, of basic texts by western historians, sociologists, and political scientists must also be added to the list.

Although not comprehensive and somewhat irregular in its coverage, UNESCO's *Index Translationum*, published annually since 1949, gives a fairly good idea of the extent of the translation activity in the various Arab states. From this listing one gains some insight into the kind of books that are being translated and, indirectly, into the interests of the Arab reading public. See Vol. I, 1949, pp. 92–96; Vol. II, 1950, pp. 273–274; Vol. III, 1951, pp. 201–203; Vol. IV, 1952, pp. 128–129, 215–217, 269–270; Vol. V, 1953, pp. 228–230; Vol. VI, 1954, p. 114; Vol. VII, 1956, pp. 145–146, 248–249, 325; Vol. VIII, 1957, p. 120; Vol. IX, 1958, pp. 111–113, 217, 303; Vol. X, 1959, pp. 136–140, 247–248; Vol. XI, 1960, pp. 418–424; Vol. XII, 1961, pp. 419–426. Of all the books listed in the foregoing indices, the majority were in the fields of literature, history, and the social sciences.

preceding. One is the staggering effect of technological change in the Arab world. The increased tempo of industrialization, the spread of urbanization, and the transformations which have resulted from these economic and social forces have affected the entire process of westernization to an extent that almost overwhelms the cultural superstructure which has been the subject of our inquiry. These trends represent an intensification of the process launched during the second phase of the encounter. They are, however, so important and far-reaching in their impact that they cannot begin to be explored here.

A second factor which distinguishes the modern phase, while an outgrowth of the technological and social forces noted above, falls more within the range of our inquiry. During the modern era the greatest popularizer of information about the West is a method the effectiveness of which could never have been anticipated by writers of the early nineteenth century – namely, the media of mass communication. Any analysis of the modern phase must place a heavy emphasis on this technique of transmitting a cultural image. Introduced initially by the Napoleonic Expedition to Egypt, the Arabic press began to play a role in the formation of public opinion and the dissemination of ideas sometime after the mid-nineteenth century. Its restricted nature, however, meant that it reached only the elite, who were also the contributors to its contents. The rate of illiteracy at the time precluded the possibility of communicating with more than the privileged few who clustered in the main cities of the Arab world. The first attempts to publish popular daily newspapers were made in Beirut (1873) and Alexandria (1876). But both were restricted in content and circulation. Low circulation rates characterized the press throughout the nineteenth and twentieth centuries. It has been only since World War II that the potential mass audience has been tapped, by a commensurate revision of format and style.[1]

The press continues to be handicapped by the fact that most Middle Easterners are still rural and illiterate. But what the press has not been able to do, radios and the cinema have accomplished. The

1. See Tom McFarland, *Daily Journalism in the Arab States*, Columbus: 1953; I. Abu-Lughod, "International News in the Arabic Press," *Public Opinion Quarterly*, Vol. 26, Princeton: 1963, pp. 600–612.

radio has entered every city and village and has become an influential factor in familiarizing an otherwise provincial audience with political and economic events in their capital and on the international scene. In the rural areas of Egypt, as well as in other Arab states, group-listening to the radio is the most prevalent leisure-time activity.

On the popular culture level, the westernizing effects of the cinema cannot be over-emphasized. Ṭahṭāwi strained his efforts to relay some vague idea about western objects and behavior patterns. But despite his somewhat laborious verbal descriptions of European clothes, food, carriages, dancing, etc., he never succeeded in bringing them to life. Now, Arabs in the smallest towns equipped with movie houses can see for themselves a wide variety of these objects and actions, set in context of value rather than objectivity.

These, then, are some of the major characteristics of the third phase of Arab-West interaction. The rapidity, intensity, and urgency of this new phase of westernization have led to new sets of reactions. It will take considerable time, however, before these can be analyzed in any meaningful sense and understood in terms of the whole context of continuous relations which now determine them.

Whatever the full picture of the present encounter and whatever the ultimate reactions to it may prove to be, the groundwork for the present was laid during the initial and tentative contact made between 1800 and 1870, prior to western occupation and intensive activities in the area. These first efforts opened new vistas to the Arabs and, in many ways, helped to determine the future orientation of Arab society. Thus, any study of the "impact" of the West on that society must take as its starting point the perhaps small but nonetheless crucial contributions made by the Arabs themselves during this early period.

Bibliography

PRIMARY SOURCES

'Abd al-Rāziq, Muḥammad A. (translator). *Nihāyat al-Arab fi Ta'rīkh al-'Arab* (Sédillot's *Histoire des Arabes*). Cairo: 1872.

Abū al-Futūḥ, 'Ali, *Siyāḥat Miṣri fi Ūrubba* (The Travel of an Egyptian in Europe). Cairo: 1900.

Abū al-Su'ūd, Ḥasan (translator). *al-Dars al-Mukhtaṣar al-Mufīd fi 'ilm al-Jughrāfiyah al-Jadīd* (A Brief and Useful Lesson in the New Geography). Cairo: 1869.

—— (translator). *Nazm al-La'āli' fi al-Sulūk fi man Ḥakam Faransa Min al-Mulūk* (The Arrangement of Gems Concerning French Monarchs). Cairo: 1841.

al-Afghāni, J. and 'Abduh, M. *al-'Urwah al-Wuthqa* (The Indissoluble Bond). Third edition. Cairo: 1931.

al-'Aqīqi, Anṭūn Ḍ. *Thawrah wa Fitnah fi Lubnān*. Beirut: 1949. English translation by M. Kerr, *Revolution and Sedition in Lebanon*, Beirut: 1959.

'Azīz, 'Abdullah (translator). *Ta'rīkh Dawlat Iṭālya* (A History of Italy). Cairo: 1833.

al-Bājūri, Maḥmūd 'Umar. *al-Durar al-Bahīyah fi al-Riḥlah al-Ūrubbāwīyah* (The Beautiful Gems in a Trip to Europe). Cairo: 1891.

Bayram, Muḥammad. *Ṣafwat al-I'tibār bi Mustawda' al-Amṣār wa al-Aqṭār* (The Purest Consideration in the Location of Countries). In Five Volumes. Cairo: 1884–1886.

al-Bayyā', lbrāhīm (translator). *Siyāḥah fi al-Hind* (Thorolde's *Travels in India*). Cairo: 1848.

al-Bayyā', Muṣṭafa M. (translator). *Maṭāli' Shumūs al-Siyar fi Waqāi' Kārlūs al-Thāni 'Ashar* (Voltaire's *Histoire de Charles XII, roi de Suède*). Cairo: 1841.

al-Bustāni, Buṭrus. *Khiṭāb fi al-Hay'ah al-Ijtimā'īyah* (An Essay on Society). Beirut: 1869.

Bustrus, Salīm (translator). *Gharā'ib al-Aqdār* (Philo's *The Wonders of Fate*). Second edition. Beirut: 1890.

—— *Al-Nuzhah al-Shahīyah fi al-Riḥlah al-Salīmīyah* (The Delightful Excursion of Salīm). Beirut: 1856.

Fikri, Amīn. *Irshād al-Alibbā ila Maḥāsin Ūrubba* (The Intelligent Man's Guide to the Beauties of Europe). Cairo: 1892.

al-Ḥarāyri, Sulaymān. *'Arḍ al-Baḍā'i' al-āmm* (Exposition Universelle). Paris: 1867.

Ḥusayn, 'Abdullah (translator). *Ta'rīkh al-Falāsifah* (History of the Philosophers). Cairo: 1836.

al-Jabarti, 'A. R. *'Ajā'ib al-āthār fi al-Tarājim wa al-Akhbār* Vol. III, Cairo: 1879. French translation by C. Mansour *et al. (Merveilles Biographiques et Historiques du Cheikh Abd el-Raḥman el-Jabarti)*, Tome VI, Cairo: 1892.

Jalāl, 'Uthmān (translator). *Riwāyat al-Shaykh Matlūf* (Molière's *Tartuffe*). Cairo: 1850.

—— (translator). *al-'Uyūn al-Yawāqiz fi al-Amthāl wa al-Mawā'iz* (La Fontaine's *Fables*).

al-Jubayli, Ḥasan (translator). *Burhān al-Bayān wa Bayān al-Burhān fi Istikmāl wa Ikhtilāl Dawlat al-Rūmān* (Montesquieu's *Considérations sur les causes de la grandeur des Romains et de leur décadence*). Cairo: 1842.

al-Kawākibi, 'A. R. *Ṭabā'i' al-Istibdād* (Attributes of Tyranny). Cairo: about 1905.

—— *Umm al-Qura* (Metropolis). Cairo: 1931.

Khayr al-Dīn al-Tūnisi. *Aqwam al-Masālik fi Ma'rifat Aḥwāl al-Mamālik* (The Best Paths to the Knowledge of the Realms). Tunis: 1867.

al-Khāzin, F. and F. *Majmū' at al-Muḥarrarāt al-Siyāsīyah* (Collected Political Documents). Jūniyah: 1910–1911.

Khilāṭ, Dimitri. *Sifr al-Safar ila Ma'raḍ al-Ḥaḍar* (The Book of Travel to the Exhibition of the Civilized). Cairo: 1891.

Maḥmūd, 'Abduh Khalīfah (translator). *Itḥāf al-Mulūk al-Alibbā' bi Taqaddum al-Jam'īyāt bi Bilād Ūrubba*. Cairo: 1841.

—— *Ithāf Mulūk al-Zamān bi Ta'rīkh al-Imbarātūr Shārlikān*. In three volumes. Cairo: 1850. (These volumes and the preceding one are a translation of William Robertson's *The History of the Reign of the Emperor Charles the Fifth*).

—— *al-Mushriq bi 'Ilm al-Manṭiq* (Dumarsais' *Logique*). Cairo: 1843.

Marrāsh, Fransīs. *Ghābat al-Ḥaqq* (The Forest of Truth). Beirut: 1866.

—— *Riḥlah ila Ūrubba* (A Trip to Europe). Beirut: 1867.

al-Marṣifi, Ḥasan. *al-Kilam al-Thamān fi al-Ummāh, al-Waṭan, al-Ḥukūmah, al-'Adl, al-Zulm, al-Siyāsayh, al-Ḥurrīyah, wa al-Tarbiyah* (The Eight Words – Nation, Patrie, Government, Justice, Polity, Freedom and Education). Cairo: 1880.

al-Najjār, Ibrāhim. *Miṣbaḥ al-Sāri wa Nuzhat al-Qāri'* (The Traveller's Lamp and the Delight of the Reader). Beirut: 1858.

al-Naqqāsh, Mārūn. *Arzat Lubnān* (The Cedar of Lebanon). Beirut: 1869.

Ni'ām, Sa'd (translator). *Siyāḥah fi Amrīka* (H. Markham's *Travels in America*). Cairo: 1845.

Qadri, Muḥammad. *Ma'lūmāt Jughrāfiyah* (Geographical Information). Cairo: 1869.

Qāsim, Ḥasan (translator). *Ta'rīkh Mulūk Faransa* (History of French Monarchs). Cairo: 1847.

Rabbath, E. (editor). *Riḥlat Awwal Sharqi ila Amrīka* (The Trip of the First Oriental to America by Yuḥanna al-Mūṣili). Beirut: 1905.

Razzāz, M. *Taṭawwur Ma'na al-Qawmīyah*, Beirut: 1957. English translation by I. Abu-Lughod, *The Evolution of the Meaning of Nationalism*. New York: 1963.

Riḍa, R. (editor). *Ta'rīkh al-Ustādh al-Imām al-Shaykh Muḥammad 'Abduh* (A biography of Muḥammad 'Abduh). Vol. II. Cairo: 1926.

Ṣābunji, Luwīs. *al-Riḥlah al-Naḥlīyah* (The Trip of the Bee). Constantinople: 1874.

Salīm, Muḥammad Sharīf. *Riḥlah ila Ūrubba* (A Trip to Europe). Cairo: 1882.

Sarkīs, Khalīl. *Riḥlat Mudīr al-Lisān ila al-āsitānah wa Ūrubba wa Amrīka* (The Journey of the Director [Khalīl Sarkīs] to Constantinople, Europe, and America). Cairo: 1893.

al-Shidyāq, Aḥmad Fāris. *Kashf al-Mukhabba' 'An Funūn Ūrubba* (Unveiling the Arts of Europe). Second edition. Istanbul: 1881.

—— *al-Sāq 'ala al-Sāq fi Māhuwa al-Fāryāq (La vie et les aventures de Fariac*). Paris: 1855.

al-Shihābi, Ḥaydar. *Lubnān fi 'Ahd al-Umarā' al-Shihābīyīn* (Lebanon during the Shihābis). Edited by A. Rustum and F. A. Bustāni. Beirut, 1933.

Ṭahṭāwi, Aḥmad 'Ubayd (translator). *al-Rawḍ al-Azhar fi Ta'rīkh Buṭrus al-Akbar* (Voltaire's *Histoire de l'empire de Russie sous Pierre le Grand*). Cairo: 1849.

Ṭahṭāwi, Rifā'ah (translator). *al-Jughrāfiyah al-'Umūmīyah* (Malte-Brun's *Précis de la géographie universelle*). In three volumes. Cairo: 1843.

—— *Manāhij al-Albāb al-Miṣrīyah fi Mabāhij al-ādāb al-ʾAṣrīyah* (Courses for Egyptian Minds in the Delights of Modern Literature). Third edition. Cairo: 1912.

—— (translator). *Mawāqiʾ al-Aflāk fi Waqāʾiʾ Talīmāk* (Fénelon's *Les aventures de Télémaque*). Cairo: 1850.

—— *al-Murshid al-Amīn Lilbanāt wa al-Banīn* (The Honest Guide for Girls and Boys). Cairo: 1872.

—— (translator). *Qalāʾid al-Mafākhir fi ʿAwāʾid al-Awāʾil wa al-Awākhir* (Depping's *Aperçu historique sur les moeurs et coutumes des nations*). Cairo: 1833.

—— *Takhlīṣ al-Ibrīz ila Talkhīṣ Bārīz* (The Extraction of Gold in the Summary of Paris). Third edition. Cairo: 1905.

—— (translator). *al-Taʿrībāt al-Shāfiyah Li Murīd al-Jughrāfiyah* (The Complete Translation for the Seeker of Geography). Cairo: 1843.

Ṭahṭāwi, R. R., *et al.* (translators). *Qānūn Yataʿallaq bi Nizām wa Tartīb al-Mashyakhah al-Baladīyah fi Bārīs* (The Napoleonic Code). Three volumes. Cairo: 1867.

Tawfiq, Ḥasan. *Rasāʾil al-Bushra fi al-Siyāḥah bi Almānya wa Swīsra* (Glad Tidings in the Journey to Germany and Switzerland). Cairo: 1891.

al-Turk, Niqūla. *Dhikr Tamalluk Jumhūr al-Faransāwīyah al-Aqtār al-Miṣrīyah wa al-Bilād al-Shāmīyah.* Edited and translated to French by Desgranges, *Histoire de l'expédition des Français en Egypte.* Paris: 1839.

—— *Mudhakkirāt*. Edited and translated to French by Gaston Wict, *Nicolas Turc, Chronique d'Egypte*, 1798–1804. Cairo: 1950.

Zaki, Aḥmad. *al-Dunya fi Bārīs* (Life in Paris). Cairo: 1900.

—— *al-Safar ila al-Muʾtamar* (The Journey to the Conference). Cairo: 1893.

al-Zarābi, Muṣṭafa. (translator). *Bidāyat al-Qudamāʾ wa Hidāyat al-ḥukamāʾ* (The Origins of the Ancients and the Guidance of the Sages). Cairo: 1836.

—— (translator). *Qurrat al-ʾUyūn wa al-Nufūs Bisiyar Ma Tawassaṭ min al-Qurūn* (The Pleasures of the Eyes and the Soul in the Beginnings of Medieval Times). Cairo: 1840.

SECONDARY SOURCES

ʿAbd al-Karīm, Aḥmad ʿIzzat. *Taʾrīkh al-Taʿlīm fi ʿAṣr Muḥammad ʿAli* (History of Education in the Age of Muḥammad ʿAli). Cairo: 1938.

Adams, C. C. *Islam and Modernism in Egypt*. London: 1933.

Ahmed, A. J. *The Intellectual Origins of Egyptian Nationalism*, London: 1960.

Amīn, Aḥmad. *Fayḍ al-Khāṭir* (Reflections). Vols. V and VI. Cairo: 1948.

—— *Zu'amā' al-Iṣlāḥ fi al-'Aṣr al-Ḥadīth* (Leaders of Reform in the Modern Era). Cairo: 1948.

Antonius, G. *The Arab Awakening*. Philadelphia: 1939.

Artin, Y. *L'Instruction publique en Egypte*. Paris: 1890.

Ayalon, D. "The Historian al-Jabarti and His Background," *Bulletin of the School of Oriental and African Studies*. Vol. XXIII, Part 2. London: 1960.

Badawi, A. A. *Rifā'ah al-Ṭahṭāwi*. Cairo: 1950.

Barbour, N. "The Arabic Theatre in Egypt," in *Bulletin of the School of Oriental Studies*. Vol. VIII. London: 1935–1937.

Bencheneb, M. "Muḥammad Bairam," in *Encyclopedia of Islam*, Vol. III. London: 1924.

Berger, M. *Bureaucracy and Society in Modern Egypt*. Princeton: 1957.

Bianchi, T. X. "Catalogue général des livres Arabes, Persans et Turcs imprimés à Boulac, en Egypte, depuis l'introduction de l'imprimerie dans ce pays," *Journal Asiatique*, Paris: 1843, pp. 24–61.

Bowring, J. *Report on Egypt and Candia Addressed to Lord Palmerstone*. London: 1840.

Bréhier, L. *L'Egypte de 1798 à 1900*. Paris: 1924.

Brockelmann, C. "Fāris al-Shidyāq," in *Encyclopedia of Islam*. Vol. II. London: 1916.

—— *Geschichte der Arabischen Litteratur*. Vol. II. Leipzig: 1902; Supplement, Vol. II. Leyden: 1938.

Browne, E. G. *The Persian Revolution*. London: 1909.

Bryson, L., *et al.* (editors). *Approaches to Group Understanding*. New York: 1947.

The Cambridge Modern History. Vol. X. New York: 1907.

Carra de Vaux. *Penseurs de l'Islam*. Vol. V. Paris: 1926.

Cattaui, R. *Le règne de Mohamed Aly d'après les archives Russes en Egypte*. Vol. I. Cairo: 1931.

Chemoul, M. "Rifā'ah Rāfi' al-Ṭahṭāwi," in *Encyclopedia of Islam*. Vol. III. London: 1924.

Cherfils, C. *Bonaparte et l'Islam*. Paris: 1914.

Coon, C. S. "The Impact of the West on Middle Eastern Social Institutions," in *Proceedings of the Academy of Political Science*. Vol. XXXIV, No. 4. Washington: 1952.

Cuinet, V. *Syrie, Liban et Palestine*. Paris: 1896.

A. Dāghir, Maṣādir al-Dirāsah al-Adabīyah, (Sources of Literary Studies) Vol. II. Beirut: 1955

Dawn, C. E. "From Ottomanism to Arabism," *Review of Politics*. Vol. XXIII. Notre Dame: July 1961.

al-Dibs, Y. *Mukhtaṣar Ta'rīkh Sūrīyah* (A Short History of Syria). Vol. II. Beirut: 1907.

Dodge, B. *The American University of Beirut*. Beirut: 1958.

Dodwell, H. *The Founder of Modern Egypt: A Study of Muhammad Ali*. Cambridge: 1931.

Duruy, J. V. *Histoire du Moyen-Age*. Tenth edition. Paris: 1880.

Fairbank, J. K. "China's Response to the West; Problems and Suggestions," *Journal of World History*, Vol. III, Paris: 1956.

Fāris, Bishr. "Aḥmad Zaki," in *al-Muqtaṭaf*. Vol. LXXXV. Cairo: 1934.

Fisher, S. N. *The Middle East*. London: 1960.

Franck, D. S. (editor). *Islam in the Modern World*. Washington: 1951.

Gabrieli, F. *The Arab Revival*, New York: 1961.

Gibb, H. A. R. *Modern Trends in Islam*. Chicago: 1947.

—— "Studies in Contemporary Arabic Literature," in the *Bulletin of the School of Oriental Studies*. Vols. IV, V, and VII. London: 1928, 1929, and 1931.

—— (editor). *Whither Islam*? London: 1932.

Gibb, H. A. R. and Bowen, H. *Islamic Society and the West*. Vol. I: *Islamic Society in the Eighteenth Century*, Parts I and II. London: 1950 and 1957.

Goldziher, I. "Djamal al-Din al-Afghani," in *Encyclopedia of Islam*, Vol. I. London: 1908.

Guémard, G. *Les réformes en Egypte*. Cairo: 1936.

Hamont, P. N. *L'Egypte sous Méhmét Ali*. Vol. II. Paris: 1843.

Hartmann, M. *The Arabic Press of Egypt*. London: 1899.

Heyworth-Dunne, J. *An Introduction to the History of Education in Modern Egypt*. London: 1939.

—— "Arabic Literature in Egypt in the 18th Century," in *Bulletin of the School of Oriental Studies*. Vol. IX, Part 3. London: 1938.

—— "Printing and Translations under Muhammad 'Ali of Egypt: The Foundation of Modern Arabic," *Journal of the Royal Asiatic Society*, London: 1940.

—— "Rifā'ah Badawi Rafi'at-Ṭahṭawi: The Egyptian Revivalist," *Bulletin of the School of Oriental Studies*, London: 1939, Vols. IX and X.

Hitti, P. K. *History of the Arabs*. Fifth edition. New York: 1951.

—— *History of Syria*. New York: 1951.

—— *Lebanon in History*. New York: 1957.

—— "The Impact of the West on Syria and Lebanon in the Nineteenth Century," in *The Journal of World History*. Vol. II, No. 3. Paris: 1955.

Hourani, A. *Syria and Lebanon*. London: 1946.

—— "The Changing Face of the Fertile Crescent in the XVIIIth Century," *Studia Islamica*. Vol. VIII. Paris: 1957.

Huart, C. *Littérature Arabe*. Paris: 1912.

Husaini, I. M. "Modern Arabic Literature," *Journal of World History*. Vol. III. No. 3, Paris: 1957.

Ḥusayn, Ṭāha. *Mustaqbal al-Thaqāfah fi Miṣr* (The Future of Culture in Egypt). Cairo: 1938. English translation by S. Glazer. Washington: 1954.

Ireland, P. (editor). *The Near East, Problems and Prospects*. Chicago: 1942.

al-Iskandari, A., et al. *al-Mufaṣṣal fi Ta'rīkh al-Adab al-'Arabi* (The Detailed in the History of Arabic Literature). Vol. II. Cairo: 1934.

Izzedin, N. *The Arab World*. Chicago: 1953.

Jessup, H. H. *Fifty-three Years in Syria*. Two Volumes. Boston: 1910.

Jomard, M. "Ecole Egyptienne de Paris," *Journal Asiatique*, Paris: 1828, pp. 109–113;

Khalafallah, M. A. *Aḥmad Fāris al-Shidyāq*. Cairo: 1955.

Khemiri, T. and Kampffmeyer, G. "Leaders in Contemporary Arabic Literature," in *Die Welt des Islam*, Band 9, Berlin: 1930.

Khūri, Ra'īf. *al-Fikr al-'Arabi al-Ḥadīth* (Modern Arab Thought). Beirut: 1943.

Kirk, G. *A Short History of the Middle East*. Second edition. London: 1955.

Kohn, H. *Western Civilization in the Near East*. London: 1936.

Kračkovskij, I. "Der Historiche Roman in der Neuren Arabischen Literatur," in *Die Welt des Islam*, Band 12, Berlin: 1930.

Kritzeck, J. and Winder, R. B. *The World of Islam*. London: 1960.

Lammens, H. *Islam – Beliefs and Institutions*. Translated by E. D. Ross. London: 1929.

Landau, J. *Studies in the Arab Theater and Cinema*. Philadelphia: 1958.

Laqueur, W. Z. (editor). *The Middle East in Transition: Studies in Contemporary History*. New York: 1958.

Lee, F. "An Arab Journalist on England," in *National Review*, Vol. LXXV, London: 1920.

Lerner, D. *The Passing of Traditional Society: Modernizing the Middle East*. Glencoe: 1958.

Lewis, B. "The Concept of an Islamic Republic," in *Die Welt des Islam*, Vol. IV, No. I, 1955.

—— "The Impact of the French Revolution on Turkey," in the *Journal of World History*. Vol. I, No. I. Paris: 1953.
—— "The Muslim Discovery of the West," in *Bulletin of the School of Oriental and African Studies*. Vol. XX. London: 1957.
—— "Some Reflections on the Decline of the Ottoman Empire," *Studia Islamica*. Vol. IX. Paris: 1958.
—— *The Emergence of Modern Turkey*. London: 1961.
al-Makhzūmi, M. *Khāṭirāt Jamāl al-Dīn al-Afghāni* (Reflections of Jamāl al-Dīn al-Afghāni). Cairo: 1931.
Ma'lūf, I. *Ta'rīkh al-Amīr Fakhr al-Dīn al-Ma'ni al-Thāni* (History of the Prince Fakhr al-Din the Second). Jūniyah: 1934.
Maqdisi, A. K. *Background of Modern Arabic Literature*. Cairo: 1939.
Mardin, Ş. *The Genesis of Young Ottoman Thought: A Study in the Modernization of Turkish Political Ideas*, Princeton: 1962.
Mathews, R. D. and Akrawi, M. *Education in Arab Countries of the Near East*. Washington: 1949.
McFarland, T. *Daily Journalism in the Arab States*. Columbus: 1953.
Menzel, T. "Khayr al-Dīn Pasha," in *Encyclopedia of Islam*, Vol. II, London: 1916.
Muel, Léon. *Précis historique des Assemblées Parlementaires et des Hautes Cours de Justice en France de 1789 à 1895*. Paris: 1896.
Ni'mat Allah al-Óarābulsi, Nawfal. *Zubdat al-ÑaÎā' if fi Uṣūl al-Ma'ārif* (Best Pages in the Foundation of Knowledge), Vol. II. Beirut: 1874.
Numata, J. "Acceptance and Rejection of Elements of European Culture in Japan," *Journal of World History*. Vol. III. Paris: 1956.
Nuseibeh, H. *The Ideas of Arab Nationalism*. Ithaca: 1956.
Penrose, S. *That They May Have Life; the Story of the American University of Beirut, 1866–1941*, New York: 1941.
Pérès, H. *La littérature Arabe et l' Islam*. Alger: 1938.
—— *Littérature Arabe moderne*. Alger: 1940.
—— "Les premières manifestations de la renaissance littéraire Arabe en Orient au XIXe siècle," *Annales de l' Institut d'Etudes Orientales*, Faculté des Lettres de l'Université d'Alger. Tome I. Alger: 1934–1935.
—— "Le roman, Le conte et La nouvelle dans la littérature Arabe Moderne," *Annales* … Tome III. Alger: 1937.
—— *L'Espagne vue par les voyageurs Musulmans de* 1610 *à* 1930. Paris: 1937.
—— "Voyageurs Musulmans en Europe aux XIXe et XXe siècles," *Mémoires de l'Institut Français d' Archéologie Orientale du Cairo*. Tome LXVIII. Cairo: 1940.

Perron, M. A. "Lettre sur les écoles et l'imprimerie du Pasha d'Egypte," *Journal Asiatique*, Paris: 1843.
Plon H. and Dumaine J. (editors). *Correspondances de Napoléon Ier*. Vol. IV. Paris: 1860.
Prisses d'Avennes and Hamont. *L'Egypte sous la domination de Méhmét Aly*. Paris: 1848.
Qara'li, P. *Fakhr al-Dīn II*. Harīṣa: 1937.
al-Rāfi'i, 'Abd al-Raḥmān. *'Aṣr Ismā'īl* (The Age of Ismā'īl). Two Volumes. Cairo: 1932.
—— *'Aṣr Muḥammad 'Ali* (The Age of Muḥammad 'Ali). Cairo: 1947.
—— *Ta'rīkh al-Ḥarakah al-Qawmīyah* (History of the Nationalist Movement). Three Volumes. Cairo: 1929 and 1930.
Richardson, J. *A Dictionary – Persian, Arabic and English*. London:1829.
Riḍwān, A. F. *Ta'rīkh Maṭba'at Būlāq* (History of the Bulaq Press). Cairo: 1953.
Rustow, D. A. *Politics and Westernization in the Near East*. Princeton: 1956.
—— "The Politics of the Near East," in G. A. Almond and J. S. Coleman, *The Politics of the Developing Areas*. Princeton: 1960.
Sabry, M. *L'Empire Egyptien sous Mohamed Ali et La Question d'Orient*. Paris: 1930.
Sāmi, Amīn. *al-Ta'līm fi Miṣr* (Education in Egypt). Cairo: 1917.
—— *Taqwīm al-Nīl* (The Nile Almanac). Vol. II, Vol. III, Part 1. Cairo: 1928, 1936.
Sarkīs, I. *Mu'jam al-Maṭbū'āt al-'Arabīyah wa al-Mu'rrabah* (Dictionary of Arabic Bibliography). Cairo: 1928.
Shahbandar, 'A. R. "Zaki Bāsha," in *al-Hilāl*, Vol. XLIII, 1934.
Shaykhu, L. *al-Ādāb al-'Arabīyah fi al-Qarn al-Tāsi' 'Ashar*. Beirut: 1924.
—— *al-Mashriq*. Beirut: 1908.
al-Shayyāl, Jamāl al-Din. *Ta' rīkh al-Tarjamah wa al-Harakah al-Thaqāfiyah fi 'Aṣr Muḥammad 'Ali* (History of the Translation and Literary Movement in the Age of Muḥammad 'Ali). Cairo: 1951.
Smith, W. C. *Islam in Modern History*. Princeton: 1957.
Sobernheim, M. "Muḥammad Bay 'Othman al-Djalāl," in *Encyclopedia of Islam*. Vol. III. London: 1924.
Ṭabbākh, M. R. *A' lām al-Nubalā' bi Ta'rīkh ḥalab* (The Notables in the History of Aleppo). Aleppo: 1929.
Tājir, J. *Ḥarakat al-Tarjamah bi Miṣr Khilāl al-Qarn al-Tāsi' 'Ashar* (The Translation Movement in Egypt During the Nineteenth Century). Cairo: 1945.

Ṭarrāzi, P. *Ta'rīkh al-Ṣaḥāfah al-'Arabīyah* (History of the Arab Press). Four Volumes. Beirut: 1913, 1914 and 1933.

Tauer, F. *et al.* (editors). *Charisteria Orientalia*. Prague: 1956.

Teng, Ssu-Yu and Fairbank, J. *China's Response to the West*. Cambridge: 1954.

Thomas, L. V. and Frye, R. *The United States and Turkey and Iran*. Cambridge: 1951.

Toynbee, A. *A Study of History*. Vol. VIII. London: 1954.

Ṭūsūn, 'Umar. *al-Bi'thāt al-'Ilmīyah fī 'Ahd Muḥammad 'Ali* (Student Missions in the Age of Muḥammad 'Ali). Alexandria: 1934.

Van Dyke, E. C. *Iktifā' al-Qanū' fī Māhuwa Maṭbū'* (The Sufficient Guide to the Contented on What is Printed). Cairo: 1897.

Von Grunebaum, G. E. *Islam, Essays in the Nature and Growth of a Cultural Tradition*, American Anthropologist, Memoir No. 81, 1955.

Young, G. *Egypt*. New York: 1927.

Young, T. C. (editor). *Near Eastern Culture and Society*. Princeton: 1951.

Zaydān, Jurji. *Tarājim Mashāhīr al-Sharq fī al-Qarn al-Tāsi 'Ashar* (Eastern Celebrities in the Nineteenth Century). Third edition. Cairo: 1922.

—— *Ta'rīkh Ādāb al-Lughah al-'Arabīyah* (History of Arabic Literature). Four volumes. Cairo: 1914.

Zeine, Z. N. *Arab-Turkish Relations and the Rise of Arab Nationalism*. Beirut: 1958.

Index

'Abbās I, Viceroy 56, 56n
'Abbāsids 154
'Abduh, Muḥammad 95n, 142n, 166n
absolutism in France 100, 101–2, 102
Abū al-Futūūḥ, 'Ali 87
Abū al-Su'ūd 64, 64n
Abū al-Su'ūd, Ḥasan 64, 64n
Abū Nazzārah 95n
Académie Française 131
Adham, Ibrāhim 61n
al-Afghāni, Jamāl al-Dīn 157–8, 166n
Al Azhar University 92, 125, 142
Aleppo 94, 147
Alexandria 27, 29, 35, 170
'Ali, Muḥammad 88n
America 80, 167, 169
American Civil War 165
American University of Beirut 166
Andalusia 83n
Anglican Church 140;
  al-Shidyāq on 137–9
'Anḥūri, Yūhanna 51n
Anṭūn, Faraḥ 70n
Arabic literature:
  stylistic changes 76–7;
  modern revival 77;
  awareness of the West means only France 167
Arabic Press 167–8, 170
Arabs:
  implications of Ottoman defeat 21;
  legacy of the past 21;
  sense of identity with the West 22;
  transformation of society 22;
  coexistence of cultural forms 23;
  deaf to radical ideas 35;
  ignorance of European events 36;
  background knowledge of educated society 68;
  Dark Ages 68;
  influx into Europe 81, 95;
  growth of awareness of the West 95;
  lack of interest pre-nineteenth century 95;
  waning interest in the Arab world 95;
  admire Europe's political ideology 162;
  appreciate literary expression of western society 162;
  recognize educational system and social organization 162;
  failure to perceive European secularism 164;
  calling for reforms 166;
  increase in literacy feeds popular press 167–8, 170
Awqāf 94, 121, 128

al-Bājūri, Maḥmūd 'Umar 86
Barrault, E; Occident et Orient 62n
al-Batanūni, M.Labīb 88n
Bayram, Muḥammad 85, 89n, 91, 92, 94
  medical visit leads to geopolitical study 149
Bedouins 20
Beirut:
  Syrian Protestant College 44, 166;
  University of St Joseph 44, 166;

Europeans in 78;
popular Arabic press 167–8, 170
Bourbon family 99, 101
Britain occupies Egypt (1882) 165
British ships 35, 62n
Būghuṣ, Yūsuf 51n
Bulaq Press 49n
al-Būstāni, Butrus 78, 141, 160
al-Būstāni, Salīm 70n
al-Būstāni, Sulaymān 70n
Bustrus, Salīm 89–90, 91, 93–4, 146;
on private associations 117

Cairo 29, 36, 37, 54n, 55, 85, 86, 87, 167, 168
Cairo University 57n
Caliphs 154, 156
Cambridge 128–9
Camus, Albert 169n
Catholic Church:
Khayr al-Dīn on 112, 130;
theology colleges 130;
al-Ṭawṭāwi on 136–7;
al-Shidyāq on 139;
and French state 140
Charles V, 74
Charles X 101
Charles XII 64, 74, 75
Charter (La Charte, Sharṭah) 101, 101n, 104, 136
Christianity:
vis-à-vis Muslim Near East 20, 164;
French invaders 36;
Arab image of 68;
Maronite students 80;
education for 130
chroniclers 142, 162
on Napoléon's Proclamations 28;
on French invasion 35–6;
on French Revolution 38–9;
on Napoléon 38, 102n;
contemporary 166n
cinema 171
Clot Bey 53
Code Napoléon 58, 67, 145
Constantinople 51, 85, 86, 87n, 92, 95
constitutionalism:
al-Ṭawṭāwi on 04–5;
Khayr al-Dīn on 108, 111–12;
Islam's natural form of government 154;
implied by the Sharī'ah 155;
attitude to 162, 163
cotton; export from Egypt 165
Crusades 152
culture-carriers:
foreigners 23–4;
indigenous 24;
European 49, 78, 165–6;
Arabs in Europe 79–80, 87–8

de Sacy, Sylvestre 93, 137
Dewey, John 169n
Duruy, Jean Victor; Histoire du Moyen-Age 157

education:
problems of personnel 48;
student apathy 48;
textbooks 48–9, 53–4;
burden of European instructors 49;
student missions 49–50, 49n, 81;
preparatory student instruction 50–1;
a continuous process not finite 125
Egypt:
occupied by French 15, 21;
appeal to Egyptian nationalism 33;
owes no loyalty to Mamlūks 33;
official state policy for translations 44–5;
Foreign Bureau 57;
Mixed Courts established (1876) 58;
centre of awareness of the West 164;
first translations of western books 164–5;
occupied by Britain (1882) 165
Egyptian:
School of Engineering 45;
School of Agriculture 47;

School of Languages (later of Law) 47, 56, 57, 62, 69n;
School of Medicine 47;
School of Mineralogy 47;
School of Pharmaceutics 47;
School of Translation (later of Languages and Administration) 47, 55
Emerson, Ralph Waldo 118
Enfantin 62n
Engels, Friedrich 169n
England:
social structure described 89;
al-Shidyāq on the government of England 114–15;
al-Shidyāq on British law 116;
al-Shidyāq on higher education 128–9;
Arabic being taught 129;
al-Shidyāq's analysis of English class structure 133–6
European:
principles of government system outlined 108–11;
private organizations 116–20;
Khayr al-Dīn on private associations 119–20;
contact with Muslims 152;
Dark Ages 156, 157

Fakhr al-Dīn al-Ma'ni 79–80, 80n
Farīd, Muḥammad 88n
Far'ūn, Yūsuf 51n
Fāṭimids 154
Fertile Crescent 44, 69, 165, 166
Fikri, 'Abdullah 58n
Fikri, Muḥammad Amīn 86, 149
France:
successive changes of government 40–1;
basic political organization described 89;
social structure described 89;
educational progress described 90, 92;
system of government 99–100;
on basic freedoms of the French constitution 103;
al-Ṭawṭāwi translates the constitution of France 103;
the concept of justice 104–5;
law and judicial procedure 104;
the intellectual heritage of the French 105–6;
principles of the French political system 107–8;
Bank of 120;
al-Ṭawṭāwi on the French Colleges 126–7;
the western approach to learning 127;
Khayr al-Dīn's comprehensive analysis of French education 129–31;
al-Ṭawṭāwi on the position of women in French society 132–3
French:
official language with Arabic 58;
al-Ṭawṭāwi on their philosophy 153
French invasion:
creates new image 21;
impulse toward change 22;
forced to retreat 27;
leaves administrative legacy 27–8;
marks end of Ottoman era 27
French Revolution 34, 36, 39, 40, 64n
admiration for military successes 41;
anti-religious tone condemned 41, 140;
repugnance of chroniclers 41;
al-Ṭawṭāwi on 100–1;
second revolution 101–2;
Khayr al-Dīn on its causes 111–12
Freud, Sigmund 169n

Germany 167
Gibb, H A R 18n, 68n, 69n, 154
Greeks 151

al-Ḥaddād, Najīb 70n
al-Ḥarāyri, Sulaymān 84, 90, 91, 147

Hemingway, Ernest 169n
Heyworth-Dunne, J 50n, 52n, 54n, 56n
Hitti, Philip K 41n, 94n
Hobbes, Thomas 169n
Homer; Iliad 70n
Hume, David 169n

Ibn Khaldūn 90, 106
imperialism 163
industrialization 149, 159, 170
Institut d'Egypte 36
Isḥāq, Adīb 95n, 166n
Islam:
dichotomy with the West 158–9;
Golden Age 163, 164
Islamic society: decline 18
Ismā'īl, Khedive 57, 58, 165
reopens School of Languages 57
Italy 79, 80, 82, 152, 167

al-Jabarti, 'Abd al-Raḥmān 29n, 32, 35–7, 160
dismisses concept 'Republic' 36;
admires French scholars and scientists 37;
deplores drunken soldiery 37, 41
Jalāl, 'Uthmān 66, 66n
al-Jinan (magazine) 160
Judaism 139

Kāmel, M 95n
Kawākibi 166n
Khayr al-Dīn al-Tūnisi 84–5, 89n
compares European and Islamic societies 90;
describes each European country 90–1;
historical breadth 91;
works reprinted 92;
urges reform on the European model 94;
warns of differences between states 98;
explains principles of European system 108–11;
on the causes of the French Revolution 111–12;
admires achievements of the Revolution 112–13;
on Catholic Church 112;
neglects events of the Revolution 112;
distressed by attacks on religion 113;
on European private associations 119–20;
comprehensive analysis of French education 129–31;
demonstrates ascendancy of Europe 147–8;
on al-shūra 154;
on previous ascendancy of Islamic civilization 156–7
Khilāṭ, Dimitri 85–6
Khūri, R 41n, 94n
Kuttāb system 50

La Fontaine, Jean de; Fables 66
Laski, Harold 169n
Lebanon:
rebellious villages 41n;
reform attempt 79–80;
frankophile attitudes 141;
and westernization 164–5;
Ottoman administration shared 166;
reform and westernization outdistances Cairo 167
Levant 81, 166
Lewis, Professor Bernard 32n, 33n, 140n
Locke, John 169n
London 62n, 118–19
L'Orient, French flagship of 120 guns 28
Louis XVI 40, 111
Louis XVIII 101

Machiavelli, Niccolò; The Prince 68
Mahmūd, 'Abduh Khalīfah 64, 65, 146, 155n, 156, 158–9
Mamlūks 29, 30
as usurpers 33, 34
Maronite Christians 80

Marrāsh, Fransīs 84, 90, 91, 94
on the French political system 98;
admires the French political system 106;
analyzes principles of the French system 107–8;
on private associations 117;
approves state support for education 129;
seeks deeper understanding 146–7
al-Marṣifi, Ḥasan 142
Marx, Karl 169n
missionaries 44, 70–1, 71n, 165–6, 166n
Molière; Tartuffe 66
Mongol invasion 154
Montesquieu, Charles de Secondat 64, 106, 113
Muḥammad 'Ali Pasha:
orders translations 15;
employs French personnel 27, 46;
first Egyptian response 43;
establishes Egyptian School of Engineering 45;
founds Miltary School 45;
launches comprehensive education program 46;
desires Egyptian state on Western model 47, 60, 75, 144, 163, 165;
student missions 49–50, 49n, 81, 169;
translation projects 51;
criticizes student translators 52–3;
concentrates translation work 54–5;
miltary and political collapse 56;
also supports non-technical books 61–2;
rewards translators 61–2;
appoints al-Ṭawṭāwi 62;
increases cotton production for export 165
Muḥammad, Prophet 30, 34, 104, 154
Muharram Bey 61n
al-Mūṣili, Ilyās Yuḥanna 79, 80
Muslims:
should accept benefical aspects of western culture 150;
contact with Europeans 152;
influence on West 152, 156–7;
need to revitalize their creativity 152;
fortunate because of their religion 153;
religion 153, 155, 158;
previously the centre of learning 155–6;
European progress depended on earlier civilization 157;
advocate westernization 164

al-Najjār, Ibrāhīm 87, 87n
Napoleon Bonaparte:
see also Code Napoléon;
occupation of Egypt 15, 21, 170;
edicts introduce European ideas 28;
Proclamation 29–32, 39;
cites alliance with Ottomans 30, 34;
French as friends of Muslims 30;
edicts to villages 31;
underlying concepts 33–5;
change from Consul to Emperor 41, 101;
becomes absolute ruler 112
al-Naqqāsh, Mārūn 67n, 82–3;
nationalism 122
Napoleon's appeal to Egyptians 30;
Arab nationalists 139;
al-Marṣifi on 142
Nūr al-Dīn, 'Uthmān 49n, 51n, 61n

O'Neill, Eugene 169n
Orientalist Conferences 86, 149
Ottoman Empire:
outmoded defences 19;
weakening of power 19–20;
corruption of officials 20
Oxford 128–9

Paris 90, 92, 117–18, 125
School of Oriental Languages 93, 131;

School of Dramatics 131
Peter the Great 74, 75
philanthropy 117–19
political aspects of Europe 98–116
see also al-Ṭawṭāwi, Rifā'ah Rāfi';
Marrāsh, Fransīs;
Khayr al-Dīn al-Tūnisi, al-Shidyāq, Aḥmad Fāris and Bayram, Muḥammad;
constitutionalism 99
Polytechnique 126
Protestantism 130, 139

Qur'ān 30, 34, 104, 153, 155

radio 170–1
reactions of the Arab 'rediscoverers':
selective adoption 150;
analysis of western history 151;
causes of Europe's ascendancy 152;
morals drawn from their analysis 152–3;
apologetics 153–5, 163;
recall the previous ascendancy of Muslim culture 155–7
Renaissance 151
republican government (Jumhūrīyah):
French understanding 29, 32, 34, 101–2;
Arab concept 32, 32n, 33n, 101
Robertson, W 155n
Roman Empire 151
Rome 80
Rostow, W W 169n
Rousseau, Jean-Baptiste 106n
Rousseau, Jean-Jacques 106, 106n, 113, 169n
The Social Contract 106
Russia 34, 98, 167

Ṣābunji, Luwīs 85
Sa'īd, Viceroy 56, 57, 165
Sakākīni, Ūghūst 51n
Ṣāleḥ, Nakhlah 85
Salīm, Muḥammad Sharīf 85
al-Sama'āni, Umays 52n
Samarkand 92
al-Sanūsi, Muḥammad al-Tūnisi 86
Sarkīs, Khalīl 86
Sarton, G 169n
Sartre, Jean-Paul 169n
secularism 139–40, 140n, 164
Sédillot 76
Sharī'ah 148, 150, 155, 158
al-Shidyāq, Aḥmad Fāris 84, 89, 91, 92
authority ensures credence 92–3;
on the government of England 114–15;
criticizes favouritism 115;
discussion of British law 116;
on English philanthropy 118–19;
contrasts French and English education 128, 129n;
on Oxford and Cambridge 128–9;
criticizes abuses of education system 132;
analysis of English class structure 133–6;
on European women 133;
contrasts English and French manners and refinement 134–5;
on Anglican Church 137–9;
on the Catholic Church 139
al-Shihābi, Ḥaydar A. 29n, 32, 35
chronicles French Revolution 39–40;
admires French military success 40
al-Shūra 154
Spain 152
Stockholm 149
Suez Canal 119, 165
Syria:
local independence 20;
leads translation movement 69, 70n;
travellers from 87

al-Ṭawṭāwi, Rifā'ah Rāfi' 33n, 60n, 61n
director of School of Translation 55, 93;
moving spirit of translation 60–1;
selects material for translation 62;
translations 65, 66;
genuine interest in the West 73;
records his residence in Europe

81, 171;
account of his stay in France 83;
first to publish 88–9, 91;
on the political organization of France 89, 98;
works reprinted 92;
on the French system of government 99–100;
on the French Revolution 100–1;
on monarchy 101;
on the second revolution 101–2;
on basic freedoms of the French 103;
translates the constitution of France 103;
on the concept of justice 104–5;
on French law and judicial procedure 104;
on the intellectual heritage of the French 105–6;
on European philanthropies 117–18;
on the subjects in a European education 123–4;
on the education of women 124;
on the pursuit of new knowledge 125–6;
on the French Colleges 126–7;
on the western approach to learning 127;
on the position of women in French society 132–3;
justification for his writings 143–4;
lists sciences which Europe is superior in 144–5;
on the Code Napoléon 145–6;
criticizes excessive belief in rationality 150;
on philosophy of the French 153;
on the time of the Caliphs 156;
distinguishes between the two worlds 158
al-Ṭarābulsi, Nawfal Ni'mat Allah 161n
Tawfiq, Ḥasan 86
theatres 82–3
Thiers 112
Toynbee, Arnold 163, 169n
Translation, Bureau of 55
divisions of 63
translations 15
central importance of 43;
independent private development 44;
selection of material 44, 60;
unorganized official interpreting (up to 1826) 45–6;
period of random translation (1826-1835) 46–54;
Muḥammad 'Ali's projects 51–3;
organized period of official translation (1835-1848) 54–6;
decline of official translation (1849-1863) 56–7;
commercial legal documents 57;
revival of the translation movement 57–9;
European legal works 58;
also belles-lettres and social affairs 59, 70;
history and biography 63–5, 69;
geography and travel 65–6, 69;
philosophy and logic 65;
anthropology 66;
literature 66;
politics 66;
law 67;
major change in subjects 69;
Syrians become important 69;
by foreign missionaries 70–1;
western jurisprudence, sociology and politics 70;
ninth century Greek legacy 71–2;
motivation for 72–3, 143;
nineteeth century neglect of philosophy of knowledge 72;
changes in methodology 76;
stylistic changes 76–7;
were first made in Egypt 164–5;
by private individuals meet greater demand 167;
from other European literature 167;
dizzying rate of translation of

western books 169
translators motivations 73–5
travellers; western orientalist 76, 78
travellers accounts:
reason for travelling 16, 78–9;
pre-nineteenth century 79–80;
influence of written records 81;
nineteenth century 81–3;
subjects of the travel books 88–91;
impact of 91–6;
inclusion or omission of phenomena 97–8;
items selected indicate cultural perception 97–8;
emphasis on organizational aspects 120–1;
belief in the organizational model 121;
note the value of Europe's education system 131–2;
unaware of secularism 139;
acknowledge western superiority except for religion 163;
from other countries than France 167;
increased travel results in new accounts 167;
more published in a decade than the past century 169
al-Tūnisi, Muḥammad 91
al-Turk , Niqūla 29n, 32, 35, 37–9
describes rise of the French Republic 38;
avoids concept of a republic 39;
deplores anti-religious tone 39, 41
Turkey; awareness of Europe 19

Umayyads 154
University of St Joseph 44, 166
urbanization 170

Vatican, the 98
Voltaire, François 106, 113, 169n
Histoire de Charles XII, Roi de Suède 64, 74, 75

Wahhābi movement 20
Weltanschauung 127
West:
intellectual ferment transforming knowledge 19;
inferior to the East spiritually 163
Westernization:
the concept 22–3;
complex sources 24–5;
commences with translations 43;
endogenous transmitters 161;
phases distinguished 161;
each increase breeds need for more 165;
'discovery' of other countries 167;
first knowledge of Europe is through French eyes 167;
variety of models gives eclectic pattern 167;
growth of hostile reaction to 168;
primacy of endogeous forces 168;
westernization of native agents 168;
effects of technological change 170;
mass communication 170;
popular culture 171
World War II 168, 170

Zaghlūl, Farḥi 58n, 70n, 95n
Zaki, Ahmad 58n, 70n, 86, 87, 91
Zaydān 58n, 67n, 70n